A Psychology
of Picture
Perception

Images and Information

John M. Kennedy

A PSYCHOLOGY OF PICTURE PERCEPTION

Jossey-Bass Publishers
San Francisco • Washington • London • 1974

A PSYCHOLOGY OF PICTURE PERCEPTION
Images and Information
by John M. Kennedy

Copyright © 1974 by: Jossey-Bass, Inc., Publishers
615 Montgomery Street
San Francisco, California 94111

&

Jossey-Bass Limited
3 Henrietta Street
London WC2E 8LU

Library of Congress Catalogue Card Number LC 72-5892

International Standard Book Number ISBN 0-87589-204-3

Manufactured in the United States of America

JACKET DESIGN BY WILLI BAUM

FIRST EDITION

Code 7343

The Jossey-Bass
Behavioral Science Series

Special Advisors

Preface

Some fields of research in psychology burst into prominence with a single study. Others congregate in the wings for some time before it becomes clear that something quite sizeable has been taking place. A psychology of pictures and perception has been gathering in that latter fashion. The study of pictures is one of those disciplines that brought puzzles to aesthetics and philosophy long before it was realized that research psychology had much to contribute, and it is only very recently that psychologists have confidently set about applying their ideas and methods to pictures. Over the last few years child psychology, cross-cultural psychology, perception psychology, and animal psychology have all added their theories and findings. It is time to bring the pieces together, to display the wealth of procedure and result, the implications for the development of perceptual skills, and the conclusions to be drawn about the perceptual abilities of adults in different cultures.

The plan of my discussion is as follows. The first or introductory chapter describes the kinds of puzzles I will investigate, the kinds of everyday pictures and recognition skills that are universal and obvious, and yet mysterious too. I will suggest that a clear, simple, readily understandable picture may tell us as much about perception as an apple falling tells us about physics. Chapter Two will describe the laws of optics that govern light, make it possible for a person to see, and make it possible for a picture to depict. Chapter Three compares different definitions of a picture, and makes predictions from the definitions that are tested, in Chapters Four and Five, against cross-cultural and cross-species evidence, studies from child psychology, and lessons drawn from pictures that deceive the eye into an impression that something represented is actually real. Chapter Six explains how classic ideas about perception, founded on a "figure-ground" phenomenon, can be reinterpreted to fit theories of picture perception. Chapter Seven shows how the figure-ground phenomenon is one case from a systematic set involving outline depiction. The rules of outline depiction are shown, in Chapter Eight, to apply to pictures showing impossible and ambiguous objects and to skills innately present in untutored blind people.

This is a work on perception, and, as is true of a great deal of recent work in perception, much of the strength of the theoretical sections is owed to James and Eleanor Gibson, who gave me a sound education (as well as much encouragement) when I was their graduate student at Cornell. James Gibson's analysis of optics and the visible environment underlies the systematic research on outline depiction reported in Chapter Seven. The themes that both the Gibsons have contributed to my work are quite obvious in the early chapters—in the first chapter where I contrast their theory of perception with a constructionist viewpoint, and in the second chapter where James Gibson's ideas about "ecological optics" are presented.

Perception and optics both need to be seasoned with philosophy if the puzzles of seeing are to become clear. It is very important to make plain that the terms in a theory are well-defined. Accordingly, there is a chapter on definitions of pictures. My debt to Nelson Goodman is not properly repaid in this chapter, for it treats a tiny and unrepresentative part of his work, and without due respect. As a member of his research group, Project Zero, at Harvard, and as a guest in his course on languages of art, I was more impressed by his work than Chapter Three indicates.

There are many demonstrations in this book which the reader can try for himself, using the illustrations. Many of the claims made and many of the explanations presented rest on the kinds of observations which the illustrations permit. I hope students will take the time to check the claims against the illustrations; understanding the claims will be easier and following the argument will be more interesting. My use of illustrations is strongly influenced by Rudolf Arnheim, whose respectful trust in his own sense of sight is a legacy to science in each of his books, and an object lesson to students in his courses. We were guests in each other's seminars at Harvard, and I must say the exchange rate worked in my favor.

Encouragement by colleagues and students has followed the growth of this book. My mentors at Cornell included the Gibsons, Moshe Anisfeld, Herbert Ginsburg, Fred Stollnitz, Erik Lenneberg, and Ulric Neisser. I learned a lot about experimental method and statistics from Thomas Ryan, at Cornell, but I have tried to hide the skeleton of statistics and experimental method that supports each conclusion in this book, for fear of deterring some students. Sara and Irving Faust, Hubert Dolezal, and David Lee were both warm and helpful during my years at Cornell.

At Harvard there was a trio of graduate students who made my seminars come alive. Morton Mendelson, Kathy Silva, and Eliot Smith, some of your spirit and acumen may have found its way into these pages. There were others too, with whom I had a fine working relationship and their names crop up in my discussions, which I think provides the best kind of acknowledgement.

Carol and Ned Mueller at both Cornell and Boston have been fine friends and helpful colleagues. At Toronto, friends and colleagues who have given me helpful comments include Paul Kolers, David Olson, Daniel Berlyne, Abe Ross, Gaynor Jones, and Gerta and Neville Moray. At the Queen's University, Belfast, I benefited more than I can say from Peter McEwan and Dick Gilbert, Robert Armstrong, Brian Scott, Raymond Brown, and Deirdre Brennan.

My wife Elizabeth translated Edgar Rubin's original Danish thesis, and searched the Royal Danish Archives for Rubin's papers. Without her aid, Chapter Six would have been impossible, and indeed without her warm support perhaps none of this work would have been possible. My son Robert's cheerful busyness has been an example to me, and if some of this book—whose writing began as he was born—is as charming as Robert it will be all worth while on that count alone.

Thanks are due to Pat Everingham for typing the manuscript, and to The Graphics Department, Scarborough College, Toronto—especially Ken Fong—for patient and thoughtful assistance with the illustrations.

I have been aided by a U.S. Navy grant to J. J. Gibson, the Milton Fund, Harvard, and a Spencer Fund Grant, Harvard, the Harvard Faculty Small Grants Program, and a grant from the Department of Psychology, Toronto. Project Zero, Harvard, of which I was a member, has been funded by the National Science Foundation and the Department of Health Education and Welfare. Some of the research reported in this work was nominated by Cornell for an American Institutes for Research Award, and was a finalist in that competition. I must thank both Cornell and the Institute for this consideration. The American Psychological Association granted me a Young Psychologists Award, in 1972, for which I am very grateful. It gave me the opportunity to visit Japan and the International Congress of Psychology in Tokyo in 1972, to talk about my work. I was given a most hospitable reception by my Japanese hosts, and I learned a great deal in talks with Kaoru Noguchi, especially, and Yoshiaki Nakajima. I have also been granted a N.A.T.O. Lectureship to visit Scotland, Ireland, Denmark, and Italy, to talk about my work and meet with colleagues engaged in related work. I must thank N.A.T.O. and say that I am eagerly expecting to learn a good deal. The Epilogue to this book closes on a note of research-to-come. Perhaps as my contacts in Europe and Japan come to influence my ideas, all of those plans will change in revealing ways. I hope so.

Toronto   JOHN M. KENNEDY
September 1973

Contents

A Psychology
of Picture
Perception

Images and Information

Chapter One

Pictures as Information

*A*s a means of communicating, pictures are as old as history, for they were among the first recording devices ever used. Pictures have been as common as the wheel and fire in past cultures, and today they are more common than ever: in magazines, textbooks, and albums, outdoors as signs, and in our homes as entertainment. As coins are to economics, pictures are to communication.

What enables a picture to communicate, to give us information? Do we recognize only pictures from our own culture? In the profusion of photographs and drawings in magazines, we may see pictures from the Stone Age alongside pictures from the twentieth century, or pictures from other countries whose languages are beyond our imitation because their roots are so different from our own. How do we react to a picture from an alien culture—say, a

1

culture whose language is totally uncommunicative to us? Often the alien picture is much more meaningful than the alien language that describes it. Often we can tell precisely what the picture depicts, even if it seems oddly stylized, or distorted, whereas the language of its maker leaves us totally perplexed. Often too we can tell the shape of a depicted object even though the object itself is foreign to us, as a photograph can show us some unusual creature from far Patagonia.

How can we tell what a picture is showing us? Can a child raised in a nonpictorial milieu recognize pictures? Unusual types of pictures might tempt a theorist to suppose that only careful training can make us understand pictures. Some pictures depict imaginary objects, such as unicorns. Some depict objects full of strange distortions, fooling the eyes and amazing the mind. Some caricatures show objects elongated, altered. These are strange representations, but are they typical? Do children need careful tutoring before they can appreciate any pictures? What lessons emerge from research in other cultures and from child psychology?

Psychology has made some progress in understanding perception of pictures and has garnered evidence from adults, children, and animals. It is my purpose to account for some ways pictures give us information, drawing on this evidence. As a background I offer a theory drawn from the psychology of perception. I apply the psychology of perception to the problem of understanding pictures. Then I pull the discussion around in a full circle by applying the lessons learned from pictures back again to the psychology of perception. In other words, my account flows from the study of perception to the study of pictures and then back again to the study of perception.

Pictures and Paintings

I focus on the idea that pictures give information, although pictures are also, of course, frequently aesthetic or expressive, and I do not wish to deny the importance of these aspects. I ask how pictures are useful for telling the observer about the location, shape, and color of an object or scene. But I am not forgetting that pictures can be attractive and provocative, that they can give pleasure and give the viewer a sense of awe at the technical skills and conceptions of their makers. Pictures can be pleasing by being balanced, rhythmic, and ornate—or by being distinctive, unusual. Pictures can fascinate, be odd, without harmony, yet indicative of something important, maybe even tragic. They can puzzle, through being contradictory.

These aesthetic qualities are undeniable, but whether a picture is aesthetic may be a different question from whether it is informative. I try to keep the two questions separate and concentrate on the second—how a picture can provide information. The other question, what makes a picture aesthetic, has been examined in fair measure (see, for example, Hogg, 1969), both as it applies directly to pictures (notably by Arnheim, 1949, 1954, 1966) and as it arises with objects other than pictures (notably by Berlyne, 1972). The aesthetics of pictures has been a rich and prominent topic for research. In contrast, the psychology of the informative uses of pictures lies scattered, its pieces needing to be brought together, introduced to one another, and reconciled if they begin to dispute each other (as indeed they will, for they are siblings who have been reared too long apart).

It may be that a psychology of information and pictures will seem helpful to aesthetics. In a narrow view, aesthetics is the study of taste and preference. In its broad sense, however, aesthetics only begins with questions of merit before ranging into all the relations between the meanings and manners of a work. Meaning and style can never be completely isolated from one another; to say where style leaves off and subject matter begins is difficult, maybe even impossible. Is the Mona Lisa a special person or are the delicate shades in which she is drawn indissolubly a part of her? If what a work shows us and the treatment by the artist belong together, then my analysis of information in pictures may reveal some of the interesting mechanics linking the effects and devices of paintings. Probably many paintings rely heavily on simply representing significant objects and features of objects, the kind of representation that I will dig into, though perhaps I will cultivate my topic more prosaically than an artist would desire.

Also, some people believe the merit in depicting anything lies in finding suitable real-world subjects and "getting them right"; they are still swayed, that is, by the feeling that paintings have to be "realistic." The maker is complimented according to how faithfully he "represents" the world, preferably in a new light. Perhaps my analysis may also show familiar things in a new way, or instill a fresh appreciation of the strange, simple, but useful skills of the cave artists, or point to some of the factors that will probably be present in any new and insightful technique for representing the world.

Although I point out some of the consistent factors in depiction, I do not think of these factors as the essence of painting as an art. Depicting objects can be a far cry from the essence of painting. Often today nothing is to be seen *in* the canvas except what is *on* it—namely, patches of paint, their color, texture, form, and arrangement. Painting, once a window on the world, is now explored as a craft in its own right, as though the artists were fixing on the glass and curtains of the window per se. Instead of Constable's landscapes, we have Mondrian's rectangles. Today picturing and painting go their separate ways. It becomes easier to realize that picturing is distinct from painting, that picturing need not have artistic merits and demerits but rather is purely a means of communicating, showing, beholding. Picturing, at heart, is a means for informing people about visible things, and that function is the subject of my account.

My goal in concentrating on the information in pictures is to provide a useful theory of depiction and a practical discussion about the ways pictures perform the workaday task of allowing us to see objects and scenes. Once the goal is reached, important issues can be faced—such as what kinds of illustrations a newly developing society might reasonably expect its preliterate adults to understand. Also, before the goal is secured, misunderstandings need to be hammered out, for traditional concepts of form and shape often prove inept when applied to pictures. Practical and theoretical problems arise when we ask how information for the shape of objects is conveyed by pictures. Indeed, a great deal needs to be said about pictorial perception—and, as is usual in any area in psychology, a great deal of work still needs to be done to test competing hypotheses. But much is now established, for example, about caricatures, pictures of impossible objects, and children's perceptions of pictures. And it happens that both recent research and recent developments in theories of form perception offer clear ideas about the informative functions of pictures. Sifting and discussing the evidence from adults, children, and animals help to separate the issues where little or no debate is necessary any longer from the issues that remain unsolved.

Studying Ordinary Pictures

To many Western adults, pictures are instantly recognizable, and one might conclude that most pictures are so obvious that understanding them is trivially easy. The temptation is to overlook skills that seem facile and to examine what is gaudy or remarkable. For example, at first, a vaudeville memory man seems more interesting than a laboratory experiment on recognition, and dramatic pictures by Dali more important than a line sketch in a geography textbook. Dali troubles our eyes and seems to require an explanation, whereas, one is tempted to conclude, the simple sketch is unambiguous and easy to recognize and so does not require an explanation.

What could be interesting about a sketch that anyone can recognize? The answer is almost paradoxical and is a lesson for every generation of psychologists: *in psychology we study the ordinary.* To understand the commonplace is one of the main aims of psychology. If we are to understand human activity, we must study that which occurs most of the time and that is, naturally, the ordinary. Psychologists must describe and explain whatever is normal, straightforward, and obvious to the man in the street. For our subject matter is people in the streets—their skills, their commonplace activities, and how they become that way, able to do what they do effortlessly and casually without a second's thought. If something is easy for an ordinary man to understand, and does not require his serious study, then we have to take this as a sign of a well-practiced skill that we should try to describe, not as evidence that the something is obvious and so not worthy of study.

For these reasons, a considerable effort needs to be made describing and analyzing ordinary pictures. Consider three aspects of line drawings, for example, to see how puzzling the ordinary can be.

First, line pictures are often only a few marks on a piece of paper. They are easy to make and comprehensible in a single glance. At the same time, they are also one of the least understood devices imaginable. How can a line (a thin ribbon of pigment) depict an edge of an object (the change created by two abutting surfaces)?

Second, in the past, the laws of vision have been explored with line displays. Often researchers paid no heed to the fact that some of the line displays they used were pictures and others were merely random markings. I try to show here that confusions have arisen precisely because researchers failed to distinguish perception of line displays as pictures from perception of the displays as non-pictorial deposits of pigment on a flat surface. A fresh analysis of line drawings allows us later to reinterpret a chapter in the history of psychology.

Third, line pictures are important in the history of psychology and have a wider history besides. In the caves of prehistory, the earliest drawings are often a mixture of painted areas of solid color (contour drawings) and heavily accented outlines. In those drawings, single lines often represent limbs or torsos or spears —exactly the same things we depict today by outline. Throughout the development of Western art and illustration, outline drawings have been present as casual preliminary sketches and as finished woodcuts or etchings—as serviceable, practical drawings and as works in their own right. From West and East, if a society has pictures, it has outline drawings. The outline drawing may be as useful and efficient a form of picturing as can be conceived. Color, texture, and size all become irrelevant, and the object is recognized in a few quick lines. Much is omitted, yet much is conveyed. The technology for making the line display is almost irrelevant—the lines can be cracks in glass, shadows on a screen, deposits on paper, cuts in wood—as long as the light to the eye is structured by the display.

Line drawings almost deserve seniority in a psychology of pictures. They are common, efficient, and as old as picture making itself. I show here that they suggest important basic visual processes —and maybe even some processes that go beyond vision, some processes common to both sighted and blind people, for I report some work on raised-line drawings that blind people can feel.

Newspapers, magazines, and comics are crowded with pictures. Billboards are displays for cars, bottles, any of a thousand objects. While leafing through a newspaper we may barely glimpse an advertisement, but in that instant we may have registered the identity, orientation, and location of the pictured things. Sometimes we read a label or caption before looking at the picture, but more often, probably, we notice the picture first and recognize the pictured object without any help from the accompanying words. As often as not, the captions could accompany any of a number of pictured scenes. All in all, it seems we do not need captions to help us identify the pictured items.

The evidence of our daily life, then, is that pictures are usually fairly precise and unambiguous in their referent. The represented objects are usually clear and specific. Guess work is unnecessary, usually. All we have to do is notice what is depicted. We normally have no impression whatsoever of anything complicated and indirect in identifying the contents of a picture—no feeling of possible uncertainty or error, no awareness of picking up inadequate clues and deducing the possible origins of the clues, no apparent need to check our identification as though the task were fraught with ambiguities and confusions. When we ask companions what they see in some pictures we are all looking at, usually they either see the same thing we do or notice other things. The point is, we rarely actually disagree (unless we are asked specifically to give interpretations or a considerable time has passed and we have to rely on memory). In the usual case, different observers are all correct, but each notices slightly different portions of the picture.

The evidence of every day is that pictures provide us with new information. Not only can we recognize familiar scenes, we can also make sense of pictures of unfamiliar things. We learn about things from pictures. We learn the form of an ardvaark, the shape of a cous-cous, the layout of the far side of the moon. Parents show the new baby in a photograph. A caricature of the President shows us how like a salesman he can be. Reference works, textbooks, encyclopedias, and dictionaries use pictures to inform the reader.

Constructive Versus Registration Theory

We do not seem to need to guess and deduce in order to understand the content of most pictures. Paradoxically, many theorists have argued almost the reverse. They say that perception in general—including perception of pictures—is very like guess work. They feel that our impression that perception copes straightforwardly with new information is somehow misleading. From their point of view, the central hypothesis is that we do guess and deduce, but for some reason we are blissfully unaware of the hard work of our senses, their guess work and their deductions. That is, supposedly, unconscious processes of inference occur in the brain prior to conscious perception.

An unconscious-inference theory was offered by Hermann von Helmholtz in the nineteenth century, and it is still a popular theory. The theory cannot be tested directly because one cannot ask an observer to describe his unconscious processes. But it is possible to consider what happens in special cases—for example, when information is provided in part but not completely and the observer is forced, willy-nilly, to guess and deduce. Such special cases are considered later.

The unconscious-inference theory contrasts directly with the impression we have of simply "registering" when perceiving. In our everyday experience, we open our eyes, look around, and simply "register" our surroundings. Some theories try to account for our ability to readily "register" the perceptible world. The theorists most closely associated with research supporting and explaining the basis for a "registration" theory are J. J. Gibson and E. J. Gibson, whose research provides the basis of several vital parts of this book.

The Gibsons' registration theory is founded on the hypothesis that perception is determined by the data available to the perceiver, not by processes that alter or supplement the available data. In contrast, the unconscious-inference theory was initially proposed on the presumption that the information available to perception is typically inadequate and perception has to supplement it. The idea is that perception may seem to be a system for picking up information, but it has to be a "constructive" system, for its data are often insufficient and imprecise.

The unconscious-inference theory and other constructive theories are popular today, as in Gregory's words (1970): "The same data can always 'mean' any of several alternative objects . . . the number of possibilities is infinite (p. 26). Sensory information is so incomplete . . . the slenderest clues to the nature of surrounding objects" (p. 11).

As a result, in the view of Neisser (1967), one should compare "the perceiver with a palaeontologist, who carefully extracts a few fragments of what might be bones from a mass of irrevelant rubble and 'reconstructs' the dinosaur that will eventually stand in the Museum of Natural History. In this sense it is important to think of perception as a constructive synthetic activity. . . . One does not simply examine the input and make a decision, one *builds*. . . . Perception is basically a constructive act rather than a receptive or simply analytic one" (p. 94).

Possibly, the foundations of this constructive view of sensory information and the resulting perceptual activity are basically shaky. The constructive theory is usually jerry-built, as it were, for the fundamental assertion that sensory information is inadequate is not established correctly. Proponents typically assert the point without describing the conditions for testing its validity, yet no meaningful theory can be asserted without stating the conditions under which the theory is to be tested. Familiar from high school science are such conditions as "NTP"—we say that X is true *if tested under Normal Temperature and Pressure*. Or "elastic limits"—Y is true *for any test made without stretching the material beyond its elastic limits*. There are relevant conditions for establishing the truth of any claim. We do not try to test the claim that "objects fall to the ground" with metal objects below a strong magnet. But the claim that sensory information is always incomplete and infinite in ambiguity is always asserted without mentioning the conditions for testing its validity.

The claim that optics provides, at best, ambiguous information is derived from the important fact (made much of by Bishop Berkeley, among others) that after light originates from a particular source it travels independently of its source, being then dependent only on the media through which it passes. Because of this fact light that has left a source can be altered by varying the media through which it passes. As a result, an identical ray of light to the eye can be produced in many ways, and any existing relationship between light and its source can be altered and yet leave the light

at the eye unchanged. A particular light ray can originate in any
of several locations or sources and it may be deviated by a lens,
reflected off a mirror, or filtered by colored glass before arriving at
the eye. How can the perceiver then assert what its true direction of
origin or type of source might have been? The conclusion is that the
science of optics is a science of ambiguity.

The conclusion that light is ambiguous about its origins is
often supported by empirical demonstrations with "distorted rooms."
Seen from one particular point of view, cleverly distorted rooms are
indistinguishable from normal rooms. Thus, the laws of perception,
once understood, can be manipulated (by artificial means) to give
false impressions. As to whether perception usually works on inadequate data, the demonstration is irrelevant. The demonstration
has to be shown to be a sample of our usual data before any claims
can be made about its being typical of anything.

The theoretical point that optics is ambiguous is conceived
in an empty way, and it is easy to see how foolish the point is if
the claim is restated as follows: If one allows light to the eye to be
infinitely alterable in its course and characteristics, then no necessary relation holds between the light and its origins. The claim is
as true as any tautology. But it is irrelevant to the daily business of
picking up information about our normal environment, where usually there are relations between light and its source. The assertion
that optics is ambiguous is foolish because our daily environment
sets boundary conditions on the behavior of light—and one must
look inside those boundary conditions to find any relations between
light and its origin. Optics *can* be ambiguous, but is it ambiguous
when circumscribed by our everyday world? That is the critical
question.

What are some conditions governing the behavior of light in
our environment? By and large, in our daily environment light
travels in straight paths from the origins to our eyes. Although in
specific pockets of the environment light is deviated from a straight
path by lenses and mirrors, these pockets are well marked by, for
example, the frames of the mirrors or the casings of the lenses or the
optical effects when the lenses are moved. As a result, light is rectilinear except in exceptional cases where optical devices are present,
and it is possible to distinguish the exceptional cases from the

simpler normal cases. Here, then, is one rule governing light in our environment. Perhaps, this one example suggests, there is a distinctive "ecology" of light and a clear-cut, orderly relationship of light to its origin.

To understand the nature of any informative relation between light and its origin, it is necessary to study the ecology of light—"ecological optics," in Gibson's phrase (1966). Rectilinear travel is one ecological condition, and there are others. The next chapter in this book describes an ecology of optics and analyzes the ways light can be informative about its origins, for once ecological optics is understood it is possible to begin to understand how a picture can capitalize on informative properties of ecological light.

The theory of perception contained in the notions of unconscious inference or constructive activity cannot be dismissed by reanalyzing the idea of optical information. The inference, or constructive, view of perception arose when it was thought that light was often uninformative, which may be mistaken, but it just might still be true that perception operates according to laws of inference and construction. Worthy ideas can arise for mistaken reasons. So it is interesting to cast a suspicious eye over the practical demonstrations that are supposed to support a constructive view of perception. For instance, what happens when information is deliberately degraded and made ambiguous—even if this is an artificial case? What happens when pictures are ill formed or incomplete? Do we "project," as a constructive view of perception would predict, a fully formed object onto the ill-formed displays? Do we see incomplete pictures as though they were complete? These are questions debated in later chapters.

Scope of Analysis

The theme of this book is that pictures provide useful information. Thus, we must first understand how anything can ever provide information and then examine how light in particular typically provides us with information. Only then can it be shown how pictures make use of the ways in which information is normally available. It is also useful to consider various definitions of a picture and then to examine some pictures in detail to see which definitions are

well conceived. Once the definitions are clarified, research evidence
on children and other cultures falls into place, and we see that the
research evidence supports one definition over another. So let us
begin by understanding the ecology of light, then philosophize about
representation, then analyze detailed characteristics of pictures and
research evidence on subjects using pictures.

A well-rounded analysis of pictures has to consider many
aspects of the problems. But it is necessary to omit some topics. To
discuss "cuts" and "pans" in motion pictures or children's understanding of "fades" and "zooms" or the processes involved in holog-
raphy and perception of holographs, or the relationship between
painting and personality, or a psychological history of art—all these
are too much, unfortunately, for one book. The basic function of
pictures is surely to allow us to see objects and scenes that are not
in our immediate surroundings, yet until recently that function was
rarely discussed by psychologists. Topics such as artistic merit, the
history of perspective, and aesthetics are treated at splendid length
however. Accordingly, I can concentrate on a neglected topic—the
informative function of pictures.

Regretably taking this one focus means neglecting the work
of many students of pictures. I have benefited from Goodman's
analysis (1968) of the ways pictures can be considered as symbol
systems, Gombrich's detailed analysis (1961) of the relationship between "knowing" and "seeing," Gardner's intriguing attempt
(1973) to place perception into an overall theory of child development, and Arnheim's work in an entire career devoted to a Gestalt
approach to pictures. These men and their works are having considerable influence in philosophy and psychology. Their ideas help
shape my analysis, but my treatment of parts of their work is all too
brief and rarely represents their major themes. But if I am to be fair
to my own theme—the information supplied by depictions—there is
not space to discuss everyone else's hobby horse, too.

The psychology of pictorial representations was neglected for
a long time by most psychologists, at the cost of some confusion in
the psychology of perception. In the 1960s picture perception as an
area of study came into its own and has begun to influence ideas
about the eyes of adults and the developing minds of children. I
hope this book will contribute to psychology in general by dealing

with questions ill considered until now, by taking an approach undeveloped until now, and by showing the profits and promise of a study of the content of pictures. It is an important fact that pictures give us information. The question for this book is—how?

Chapter Two

Light as Information

*H*ow does a picture give us information? Let us first sketch some principles that help explain how light operates in our environment, for we may best begin to understand how a picture provides information by first understanding how information is generally available. We will consider two propositions that arise from common observation.

The first proposition is that we are generally accurate in our perception of the physical, geometric arrangement of our world. We can tell where things are in relation to each other and to our own body without much trouble or error. In these matters, the senses are generally truthful. We sometimes overlook something, but we rarely misperceive. Accurate perception is so much the rule that we almost never think about it; instead, we treat any errors as odd and interesting because the incidents are unusual. (Beginning students are often lead into errors of perception, with illusions, in order to convince them that the problem of perception is important—as though the accuracy of perception is uninteresting once it is brought to our attention!) We live with accurate perception the way a fish lives with water, relying on it, trusting it, rarely needing to think about it.

The second proposition is that we do not need to make immediate contact with the objects that we seem to perceive so accurately. Eyes do not have to be adjacent to the things they see and ears do not have to be pressed to every sounding instrument. In these matters the senses are at one remove from their targets. Somehow, from a distance one can find out about objects and be quite accurate.

The problem set by the two propositions is this: How can perception be consistently accurate and yet operate at a distance from objects? J. J. Gibson (1950, 1966) of Cornell University has tried to answer this question, and his work forms the basis for my discussion.

How could accurate information ever be available? Light travels considerable distances before the eye receives it. A single ray of light could have been emitted by a source at one inch, one mile, or one light-year from the eye. Is that spot of light a pinprick in a nearby screen, or is it a star in distant space? Those two spots of light separated by a few seconds of arc—are those close together, or are they as far apart as the planets?

In principle, the question is: Which properties of light provide information about light sources? To begin to answer, we must first establish conditions under which anything can be said to be informative about anything else. Starting with a subject other than optics, let us imagine that a radio has been taken apart, with its switches and resistors lying to one side and its case to the other. Now, is there anything about the switches and resistors that is useful information about their previous location in the radio? Imagine that each switch and resistor is labeled *A, B, C,* and so on. If each switch and resistor has a different label, and each location in the radio case has its own label (location *A*, location *B*, and so on), there is information on the switches and resistors about their previous locations. If each part is labeled differently, complete information is provided. The labeling is unequivocal; if some of the parts are labeled similarly—say, there are two parts marked *A* but only one location *A*—there is some ambiguity. If all the parts are labeled identically, there is no information in the labels about their previous locations.

Labels are informative when they are unequivocal, just as words are informative when they are unambiguous. Similarly, in optics, a light pattern could be said to be informative about its origin if the light could have come from one particular origin and no other. At this point, it is easy to see why many authors reached the conclusion that light must be full of ambiguity: Could not the light have come from any distance, or from a picture of an object, or have been reflected off a mirror? This conclusion is unsatisfactory; it flies in the face of the accuracy of everyday perception. Light cannot be endlessly ambiguous; if it were, vision would make endless errors.

The Environment and Light

To show how light can be informative, let us consider the kinds of origins light comes from in our normal environment.

The Environment. In general terms the environment is a "terrain" dotted with "objects," changing in time to create "events." The *terrain* is the general *surface* of the terrestrial globe, and surfaces are boundaries between substances, often boundaries between the air and solid material. The *objects* in the environment are enclosed volumes of matter, the boundaries of objects being their surfaces. The *events* that occur in time are usually changes in the surface of the terrain or movements of the objects on the terrain. In general, events are changes in the properties of the environment.

Light. Most surfaces are enclosed in the transparent medium we call air. Surfaces can reflect light in any direction in which there is a transparent medium. The reflected light passes through the transparent medium, maintaining its original direction until there is a change in the medium. The light traveling through a transparent medium is "available" to a perceiver, ready for him to use if he puts his eyes at the right place. The places at which light is available can be thought of as points, called either *points of observation* or *station points.* (Either of these terms, derived from projective geometry, may be used, though "station point" is sometimes used only when a picture is present and "point of observation" only when an observer is actually present.) These points at which light can be registered are places to which light comes from the terrain. The light passes through the point and continues without deviation. (Station points do not make light informative; the light coming to the point has its own characteristics, such as color and direction. Station points are just places. Station points all treat light identically, and differences in the light at different station points result from the different origins of the light.)

Optic Arrays. The light from the surfaces of the environment converges to a station point, passes through it, and diverges away from it. We shall consider only the convergent illumination, for, of course, anything true about the convergent illumination would be true of the divergent illumination, too. The convergent illumination has intensity and "color" (spectral composition), and we can measure the intensities of light from various directions or measure the wavelengths (spectral composition) of light from various directions.

In addition to intensity and spectral composition, the convergent illumination has a *structure* that is independent of intensity or spectral composition. The light from one direction and the light from an adjacent direction may be different, in which case there is a *contrast,* and the arrangement of contrasts is a pattern or structure that is independent of the intensity or color of the light. The same structure could be present with different intensities and spectral compositions—for example, raising the intensity of illumination does not change the structure. When the sun comes out from behind a cloud, the landscape brightens, but it still looks like the same place. And subtracting light uniformly from all the convergent illumination would not change the structure. Donning sunglasses can make a scene less glaring, but the same pattern is visible.

The structure or pattern made by the contrasts is called the optic *array*—the scene is "arrayed" before our eyes. The optic array at a station point is *ambient,* since it fully surrounds the station point. In general, the optic array is the arrangement of all the differences of illumination that arrive at the station point. The basic conception of the optic array is made more useful when three important points are added, as follows.

First, the optic array is not just an optic structure at a given moment, not just a frozen pattern. There can be structure across time, too, because of changes as time passes. From one moment to the next, light patterns may change. Usually the light patterns change when the point of observation is shifted. If a part of the terrain moves, that usually creates changing light patterns, too.

Second, the contrasts of an optic array enclose three-dimensional angles called *solid angles* to distinguish them from plane angles, which exist in two dimensions. Where there are many contrasts in the optic array, the optic array can be said to have an *optic texture*. Just as a surface may be stippled by many spots of color and have a surface texture, a station point may have many contrasts and have an optic texture.

Third, optic contrasts are one kind of *optic discontinuity*, this being a general term for any kind of abrupt change. Optic discontinuities include abrupt change in the kind of optic texture present in the optic array, and abrupt change in the density of optic texture. An abrupt change in light from one moment to the next is another kind of optic discontinuity—a discontinuity in time.

Optic Arrays and Their Origins

Now that some features of the environment and its light have been described, we can face questions about information and ambiguity. The basic question is: Are there properties of optic arrays that are informative about their origins in the environment? To answer this, we must show that some aspects of an optic array are related only to certain, not all, aspects of the environment. Paraphrasing G. A. Miller (1951), origins may change and light may change, but can we show that change in one is linked to change in the other so light can be informative? Let us reexamine the description given so far.

Information for Direction of Origins. Light leaving a surface maintains its direction in a uniform medium. In an environment swathed in a uniform medium like air, adjacent elements of an optic array come from adjacent directions (Fig. 1), and the direction of any source is the direction its light comes from. To that extent, there is some information for direction in an optic array. As the direction of the origin changes, so will the direction of the light from it, if the medium is uniform.

However, adjacent solid angles may not have come from adjacent surfaces. In Fig. 1, areas A and B, two surfaces in the environment, project adjacent light to a station point. Areas B and C also project adjacent solid angles of light. But only B and C are adjacent surface areas. Area B is nearer to the station point than A. It seems that the relative distances of surfaces can be ambiguous despite the presence of information for their direction. Optical adjacency—the adjacency of two optic angles—does not specify material adjacency, which is the adjacency or continuity of the surface areas from which the light originates.

Information for Adjacency. It is necessary to look a little beyond optic adjacency for information for adjacency, for there are conditions under which two adjacent solid angles will have come from two adjacent parts of the environment. As Fig. 2 suggests, surfaces are typically somewhat homogeneous in texture. That is, surfaces usually show some regular distribution of patches of color, and usually too there is also some regular distribution of the corrugations—minor indentations and elevations—of the surfaces. (J. J. Gibson, 1950, pointed out that surfaces are usually textured. Metzger, 1936, showed that texture seems critical in how one perceives an area as a surface. Beck, 1966, showed that areas of different texture are quickly distinguished even if they are on the same plane and are the same color. Brodatz, 1966, has made an important set of photographs of surfaces, with each photograph of a different surface showing unique surface texture. Brodatz includes some black-white reversed prints along with normal prints; the textures of the normal prints and the reversed prints are the same and even a brief inspection shows that the surfaces are clearly of the same type.)

What follows if surfaces are textured? If it is true that surfaces are typically regions of the same kind of texture, then abrupt changes (discontinuities) between kinds of texture will usually occur only when there is a change in the material of the surface. The related light—containing an abrupt change or discontinuity of optic texture—provides optic information for the change of surface. It

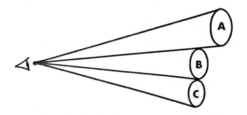

FIGURE 1. Areas A, B, and C project light to the station point; B and C touch each other, while A is quite separate, though the light from A adjoins the light from B.

FIGURE 2. Each of the separate surfaces shown here, has, schematically, its own distinctive, fairly homogeneous texture. Perhaps most natural substances and many artificial substances have distinctive but evenly distributed textures.

follows that regions inside texture discontinuities are usually regions of continuous surface. So any light within a discontinuity of optic texture has come from a continuous surface. *Adjacent solid angles in the optic array that are enclosed within a discontinuity of optic texture come from adjacent surface areas.*

Thus, there is information in optic arrays about the direction and adjacency of parts of the environment. Perhaps there is information for other properties of the environment—for instance, the distance of parts of a surface from the station point. Areas may be adjacent to one another, but is one further from the station point than another?

Since the shape of an area (its silhouette) is often considered of primary importance to perception, it may be helpful to show some problems in using shape to understand relative distance of parts. Consider a discontinuity of optic texture in an optic array. The discontinuity will have a particular shape. Now a particular surface area projects a particular solid angle to a given station point, but the shape of that solid angle could be projected by many different surfaces in the environment. In Fig. 3 various surfaces show all manner of slants and hence all variations of relative distances of parts. Some slant back, some slant forward, some are curved, and some are flat; but the shape of the solid angle of light they project to the station point is the same in every instance. So it may be difficult to use the shape of a particular solid angle of light as information for its origin.

Some of this ambiguity would evaporate if we knew all the possible shapes of all the possible origins in our environment. If we were familiar with all the possible shapes of objects, we might be able to make some good guesses about the origins of a pattern of light. For example, if it happened that all four-sided figures were squares, then any time a four-sided pattern of light appeared, the origin would have to be a square. Alas, objects have almost endless shapes. It may be best to turn to something that cuts across all types of shapes. Is there anything that is part of our perceiving just about any shape? Perhaps. If shapes are made of materials with definite surfaces, and surfaces are textured, then shapes are textured and perhaps once again texture may be useful.

Information for Slant. Solid, worldly objects have shape by having surfaces that are moulded and sculpted into facets that slant this way and that. If they are textured, these surfaces could provide information for slant—that is, relative distance of parts of a surface with respect to a station point—as follows. Each element of texture on a surface projects a solid angle of light to our eyes, and if the surface is uniformly textured, the average size of its texture elements is the same all across the surface—on areas near a station point and areas far from a station point. So, by and large, distant surface elements project smaller angles of light, and as the surface slants away from the station point, the projected optic texture becomes more densely packed, as Fig. 4 shows. Therefore, the parts of the surface projecting small, densely packed optic texture elements are further away from the station point, thus yielding infor-

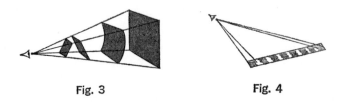

Fig. 3   Fig. 4

FIGURE 3. Differently shaped and slanted surfaces can all project the same solid angle of light, so it may be difficult to use the shape of a solid angle of light as information for its origin.

FIGURE 4. Texture on distant parts of a surface projects smaller angles than nearby texture on the surface.

mation usable by the eye (as Braunstein (1968) showed). The rule, then, is this: *If the environment is composed of regularly textured surfaces, then the relative distance of parts of the surface from the station point is specified by information in the optic array.*

Information for Separation of Surfaces. So far, I have shown that light tells about two things: adjacency and relative distance of parts of one continuous surface with regular texture. To take the analysis a step further, consider two distinct surfaces. Does an optic array yield information for the relative distance of two separate surfaces? As Fig. 5 shows, one surface may be nearer to or farther from the station point than is another surface and still give rise to the same optic array. How can this ambiguity be bypassed? This is a very practical problem that arises, for example, when aerial photography is used to map a region.

It would not be wise to try to describe and evaluate here all of the possible solutions to the problem. But there is one basis that seems reliable in theory and in practice, which can be firmly rooted in the description of the environment used so far, and a careful description of it will allow me to make a number of logical points later. Since I will describe only one basis for solving the problem, my discussion will not represent much of the usual psychology of perception, but my purpose is to show the logic of a view of information, not to offer a comprehensive theory.

The solution I want to use is simply this: The ambiguities shown in Fig. 5 remain only so long as one solitary point of observation is considered. Let the observer move or look with two eyes obtaining information across time or across space, and the ambiguities in Fig. 5 disappear. As Fig. 6 shows, parts of a surface that are not visible at one point can be seen from a nearby point. Put technically, the part that is only projected to one station point is

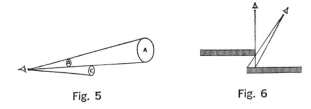

Fig. 5   Fig. 6

FIGURE 5.   The same optic array can be projected by surfaces at various distances.

FIGURE 6.   Parts of a surface not visible from one station point may be visible from another. If the observer moves from one station point to the other, the hidden surface texture would gradually appear, element by element.

said to be *occluded* from the other station point (Kaplan, 1969). The more distant surface has some of its area occluded by the nearer surface. With gradual movement of the station point, the occluded area gradually appears, texture element by texture element. As Kaplan puts it, there is gradual "accretion" of texture elements in the optic array showing which surface is more distant. The texture elements are "deleted" gradually if the direction of movement is reversed. Accretion and deletion of texture shows which of the two surfaces is more distant. To repeat, in the relation between two arrays at two station points there can be information for the separation of two surfaces and for which of two surfaces is more distant.

Direction, adjacency, slant, and relative separation—these basic aspects of layout—all seem to be specified by properties of light, provided what I have said about surfaces having texture holds true. Optic arrays need not be hopelessly ambiguous about the origins of light in the environment. Briefly put, the three key points are as follows:

First, information for the direction of sources is present, provided that the illumination from environmental surfaces travels in uniform media, maintaining its direction.

Second, information for the adjacency of surface areas is present, provided that continuous stretches of surface of one material are uniformly textured.

Third, information for the separation of surfaces is present across optic arrays.

This analysis of the information in light is a promising beginning because it shows how a theory of perception needs a description of the environment and a careful description of optic arrays. Let us now try to fit depiction into the analysis.

Depiction and Information

We will begin with a puzzle. The whole notion of optical information depends on the condition that some properties of light are unequivocally related to some properties of the environment. If the environment can be pictured, then the light can come from two sources, the usual origin or a picture. But this threatens the idea that light is informative because it can have only one kind of origin.

Of course, pictures might not give information of the kind discussed so far. Pictures might be conventions, subject to fashion and momentary canons of whatever educational fancy was enforced. If so, pictures would be more like language than like light, more like a complex system of invented rules than like a device rooted in the optics of the environment. But if pictures are like language, how is it that we have machines that "take" pictures, but not machines to "take" names? Surely pictures provide information in a way that is unlike language, a way that makes use of the laws of light as cameras do. If so, the puzzle is how to introduce a concept of picturing into a theory about information in light and keep the theory consistent.

Let us rethink the basic terms. It has been shown that across station points there can be information for the relative distance of surfaces. It follows that if an observer is restricted to a single station point, then he may have no basis for determining which of two surfaces is nearer. Many arrangements of surfaces could then provide the particular array available to the observer. The observer could be restricted even more: Any information that depends on the texture of surfaces could be degraded or withheld by the use of special filters or by painting over the surface and hiding its texture. These circumstances could remove information about the slant of the surface, and the origins of the optic array would become quite ambiguous. Restricting the observer and changing the normal environment can *create* ambiguity where once there was faithful information. Also, it is possible to artificially create an alien texture on a surface. Scattered deposits of pigment can be painted on it. A texture can be cast on it with multiple shadows. The surface could be cut many times to give it a texture of grooves and cracks. This artificial texture could be on a surface equidistant at all points from an observer and yet create an optic texture normally coming from a slanted surface in a world where surfaces are uniformly textured.

The point here is that an optic array is physically distinct from its origins. Light can be manipulated independently of its origins. The origins themselves can be artificially treated to change the typical relations between optic arrays and their origins. Think of it this way: A kind of artificial source of light may have entered our ecology when man first made cave paintings. The new kind of source of light may have become more common and more important with each step along the way to photography, motion pictures, and television. The result may be that, for us to understand optic information, it may be best to distinguish "artificial" sources from "natural" sources at the outset. (The most useful criterion for making the natural/artificial distinction may be intervention by direct human action. The result of human action is that there are not only natural surfaces with regular texture but also artificial surfaces with irregular textures, or, like some plastics, no texture at all.) The difference between natural and artificial sources is not easy to define, but the precise definition is not of pressing importance now. The question is, what kind of theoretical value would the natural/artificial distinction have? Would it be useful for understanding picturing?

The argument could be as follows: There is information in light in a natural environment, in which surfaces are regularly textured. A naturally occurring optic array, originating in a natural environment bathed in a uniform medium, is informative about its origin. Man occasionally intervenes in the natural order of things. Man produces some artificially treated surfaces that yield information for differently arranged natural surfaces. The artificially treated surfaces *represent* or *picture* or *depict* other layouts. Hence, the concept of information is compatible with a concept of pictorial representation, for one is based on natural surfaces and the other on artificial surfaces.

The laws of optic information have to be established using one set of surfaces—the natural surfaces—and then pictorial representation is allowed for by acknowledging a second set of surfaces (so-called treated surfaces), which follow slightly different rules. The natural and the artificial sets of surfaces are closely related, but that does not mean that an observer necessarily has trouble distinguishing them. For example, someone might paint a continuous flat surface so that it provides an optic array like one from two or more separated surfaces. But if the observer moves, the flat surface will not provide accretion-deletion information, whereas the separated surfaces would. Any observer who can deal with optic information from a static, motionless world should be able to accept information from the flat artificial surface. If the observer can use information across time, he should be able to distinguish the artificial case from real separated surfaces, and not confuse the two. Therefore, any observer who can use static information and kinetic information should understand the picture without confusing it with reality.

In summary, light is lawfully related to its origins and provides useful information about the world. The lawful relations between light and its sources allow pictorial representations to be created; that is, one layout of surfaces can be artificially treated to provide information for a different layout. The argument suggests that any organism that uses optical information should understand pictures. But there is an alternative to be borne in mind. It may be that many sketches violate the proposal that most pictures use naturalistic optical information. How will a theory based on optical information account for caricatures and outlines? Caricatures do not show us naturalistic shapes. Outline drawings omit all the naturalistic color and texture of the world. Then, too, don't most animals ignore even moving pictures? Aren't pets indifferent to television? Don't "primitive" peoples misunderstand photographs? Pets and "primitives" are as able to see as any Westerner, so if they fail to understand pictures a new theory is needed. Also, how can a theory of representation be based on the optics of our environment and yet deal with images of unreal, imaginary events that never existed in our environment? The theory of optics and information and representation may not work in practice. The evidence may be negative when each implication is tested against hard facts.

Indeed, the theory is a delicate affair of promises and might-be's. Most of the properties of light that are informative remain unknown (Freeman, 1965; Epstein, 1967). The ways in which the eyes rely on light are mysterious (Gyr, 1972). The kinds of pictures that are judged to be good representations are not always what the geometer or physicist would predict (Pirenne, 1970). In many cases the problems may mean that a few minor adjustments need to be made to the rough basic ideas. But the reason for adjusting and perfecting a rough idea should be that its major implications hold true and that no other ideas explain the evidence. Do the major implications of ecological optics stand the test of research? Is there a better theory of pictures? In the next chapter I will outline some competing theories, and later chapters will challenge them with evidence.

Chapter Three

Four Theories
of Pictures

*I*s a perceiver constructing his perceptual world, or is he simply registering the perceptible world? The environment might be available to us in light, like a faithful attendant. Or it might be, at best, ambiguously hinted at, only suggested in vague and often misleading sensory patterns, and never conclusively manifested. Allied with these conflicting views of perception are conflicting definitions of pictures, whose implications and logic need to be sifted.

Can any one view of pictures deal with all kinds of pictures? Think of the diversity of pictures! Line drawings are so clear yet omit so much of the represented scene—the color and texture, for example. Caricatures are fascinating because they present something in a new and odd way. Some pictures are as sketchy as a few spots of ink, but can be seen as butterflies or balls or hoops.

One might expect that most views on the nature of a picture would apply well to some kinds of pictures. The question is do some views apply to many kinds of pictures and also suggest research to support them? If so, it will be apparent which views deserve close attention, as each kind of picture is considered.

The many ideas about picturing, however, can be summarized (with only a little violence) as variations on four major themes: first, that pictures are simply conventions, no more related to what they represent than alphabetic writing; second, that pictures are simply similar to what they depict; third, that pictures provide the same elements of light as the represented objects or scenes; fourth, that pictures provide the same optic information as the pictured objects or scenes.

Each of these views deserves our careful consideration, and to begin with it may be useful to restate the fact we want to explain. Some surfaces, on inspection, allow observers to describe things that are not present. On being confronted with such surfaces, observers mention arrangements of surfaces and features of surfaces that are simply not present before them. The observers say they "see" these absent arrangements of surfaces. They can usually say accurately that some things are really present (for example, a flat surface at some particular distance) and the other arrangements of surfaces (for example, the shapes of unicorns) are not really present. And observers usually say that they are looking at "a picture of a scene." Such pictures are produced by arrangements of pigment deposits on a surface (as in paintings or drawings), or patterns of shadows on a surface (lantern slides), or configurations of grooves and scratches on a surface (etchings). Where the pigments or shadows or grooves allow perception of scenes that are not present, pictorial perception or *indirect* perception (Gibson, 1954) can be said to occur.

In some cases a display made of scratches or shadows or deposits of pigment is simply reported as a flat pattern, without any mention of an absent scene. In such cases, pictorial perception is not occurring, only *direct* perception (Gibson, 1954) of the surface and its characteristics. The neutral term *display* is useful for describing any artificially treated surface, with its pigment traces or shadows or grooves. Only some displays are representational; only some displays allow "pictorial" perception of something other than themselves.

What is the nature of a display that allows pictorial perception? Let us consider four conceptions.

Arbitrary Convention

Consider a circle. Observers say that it can be seen as a drawing of a ball, a coin, a hole, a lake, or the top of a round peg in a round hole. It is worth taking the time to look at length at a circle, to check that each of these referents can indeed be represented by a circle in a way that is quite unlike the way words stand for their referents. Notice that each time a new referent comes to mind, in some odd way the circle may even seem to alter its appearance a little, while, of course, it clearly also remains physically unchanged. In Chapter 8, even more striking changes of appearance are shown by simple pictures such as a four-sided figure that can look like a kite or a sail. Other examples of simple figures that convey many impressions are easy to come by. Readers might find it useful to draw a few to make their own observations.

An element of choice or instruction seems to be involved in the appearance of the circle seen as a picture. Small wonder, then, that many theorists opt for the view that pictures are simply conventions. Accordingly, one view is that no pictures have an intrinsic relation to that which they represent. In this view, pictures depend wholly on some social convention. Steinberg (1953) argues that technical skill in imitating nature simply does not exist, and what does exist is the skill of reproducing handy graphic symbols by set professional conventions. Arnheim (1954) comes very close to this view when he argues (pp. 117–19):

"As a rule in a given cultural context the familiar style of pictorial representation is not perceived at all—the image looks simply like a faithful reproduction of the object itself. [To trained observers] the Picassos, the Braques, or the Klees look exactly like the things they represent. Anyone who is concerned with modern art will find it increasingly difficult to remain aware of the deviations from realistic rendition that strike the newcomer so forcefully. . . . As far as the artists themselves are concerned, there seems to be little doubt that they see in their works nothing but the exact equivalent of the object. . . . Pictorial representations that come from the observer's own cultural environment appear to him as "styleless," that is, as done in the only natural and correct way."

Not as extreme as Steinberg, Arnheim argues that it is possible for an object to share significant aspects of form with its portrayal. But many of his statements do verge on the view that representation depends more on the observer's attitudes than on the picture itself. And in this, Arnheim, a psychologist, shares a great deal with Steinberg, an essayist, and also with a significant movement in contemporary philosophy, anchored in the work of Nelson Goodman.

To Goodman, realistic representation "depends not upon imitation or illusion or information, but upon inculcation. Almost any picture may represent almost anything; that is, given picture and object there is usually a system of representation . . . under which the picture represents the object and there are usually many such systems" (Goodman, 1968, p. 38). He adds that representation is a matter of choice and "realism is a matter of habit," and, of course, the choices and habits are the observer's, not something inherent in the picture. Goodman's position is not a simple one, for he suggests that, in "selected and familiar respects," judgments of similarity may be as objective as any other judgments about the world. Thus, in Goodman's analysis there is a possibility that some pictures might be found to be closely allied with their subject matter. Be that as it may, Goodman says "the criteria of resemblance vary with changes in representational practice" (p. 39). And "the plain fact is that a picture, to represent an object, must be a symbol for it, stand for it, refer to it . . . almost anything can stand for almost anything else" (p. 5).

Arnheim's theory of pictures is a bold attempt to deal with artistic merit. Steinberg's concern is the canons of progress in artistic movements. Goodman's aim is a set of clear definitions of systems of symbols, and modes of representation. Of the three, Arnheim's theory of perception is the most sensitively conceived, being an attempt to describe the fusion of thought, imagery, and vision evoked by paintings. Both Steinberg and Goodman offer quite stark assumptions about perception. Neither Goodman nor Steinberg believe that the light to the eye of an observer leads to a determinate perception, and their conclusions are quite like Gregory's (1970), discussed in Chapter One. To Steinberg (1953) an ecology of optics and picturing would be ill fated, for the eye is "hopelessly involved in mysterious cerebral operations." To Goodman, "just as a red light says 'stop' on the highway and 'port' at sea, so the same stimulus gives rise to different experiences under different conditions" and, at least so far as pictures are concerned, "the behavior of light sanctions neither our usual nor any other way of rendering space" (p. 19). Like Arnheim, Goodman thinks that Picasso one day may be called a painter of likenesses and tells the story that when Picasso heard the complaint that a portrait did not look like its subject, Gertrude Stein, he replied "No matter; it will" (p. 33).

The theory that pictures are based on conventions can explain the variety of a circle's depictions as merely a set of one culture's arbitrary choices. Western observers have been trained in an accidentally chosen set; the circle is no more a proper depiction of a hoop or a hole than the word "bow" is a proper term for posture or clothing or archery equipment. The theory carries the testable hypothesis that different cultures and untrained children would not see a circle as having the same kind of referent as adults in our culture. Indeed, Goodman recognizes with satisfaction that Herskovits, an anthropologist, says ethnographers have reported "the experience of showing a clear photograph of a house, a person, a familiar landscape to people living in a culture innocent of all knowledge of photography . . . to have the picture held at all possible angles, or turned over for inspection of its blank back, as the native tried to interpret this meaningless arrangement of varying shades of gray on a piece of paper" (Herskovits, 1948, p. 381). Cross-cultural evidence will have to be considered carefully, later, to see if Herskovits has come to the correct conclusions.

Surely the whole thrust of the convention theory runs counter to everyday experience, however much the ambiguity of circles or reports by ethnographers might lend it support. After all, pictures are used to give information. People and places not known to readers are depicted in textbooks and newspapers. Something is being transmitted by illustrations, for students make correct identifications of real things by matching the illustrations with their referents. At least some pictures may be more than mere conventions.

The convention theory is essentially negative; it argues that there is no relation beyond the arbitrary between pictures and represented scenes. The usefulness of illustrations suggests more definite relations may hold. Why else would pictures be used to supplement text? So a start should be made toward tracking down some relations that may hold for at least some pictures, in at least some cultures. A beginning might be made with the simple view that pictures often "resemble" their subjects.

Similarity and Pictures

We often say that a picture is a good or bad likeness. Photographers usually take our pictures from many angles and in many lightings to make sure they get a "true likeness." The photographer, as much as the portrait painter, knows what he is looking for only in very general terms; he has no sure way to define or to capture that much-desired likeness. Both photographer and painter agree with some schools of philosophy that "resemblance" or "similarity" or "likeness" is the key concept in depiction.

Peirce, Ogden and Richards, Morris, Wittgenstein, and Langer, philosophers with diverse points of view, all agree that representational pictures are "like" or "are similar to" what the represent.

In his earlier writings Peirce defined pictures as "likenesses" and later (1940) he called them "icons" or "simulacra." An icon "refers to the object that it denotes merely by virtue of characters of its own, and which it possesses, just the same, whether any such object actually exists or not." The icon does not match that which it represents in all particulars; representation is always "in some respect or capacity" rather than in all respects. A representation has "common qualities" with its object.

Ogden and Richards (1946, p. 12) treat images briefly; these are "more or less directly like the referent." Morris writes that an icon, in Peirce's sense, "has the properties of its denotata," and by denotata he means the thing represented. Like Peirce, he argues that not all of an icon's properties are relevant: "A sign which is to some extent iconic may itself have properties which are not iconic and which are not relevant to its signification" (1946, p. 23). Thus, he says, an icon is "similar in some respects to what it denotes" (p. 191).

Wittgenstein (1961, p. 15) argues that a picture "must have something in common with what it represents. There must be something identical in a picture and what it depicts, to enable the one to be a picture of the other at all." Langer (1951, p. 68) notes that an outline picture shares "a certain proportion of parts" with its object and that "the only characteristic that a picture must have in order to be a picture . . . is an arrangement of elements analogous to the arrangement of salient visual elements in the object."

Being "like," having "common qualities," or "resembling," being "analogous with," being in some part "identical to" the represented scene—a variety of terms pointing toward the idea that when an observer looks at a picture he picks out a distribution of material that is the same as the distribution of materials in the represented scene. Langer is the most precise in that she does not simply speak of sharing qualities but offers a specific shared property named "proportion of parts" and "analogous arrangements of elements."

However, there are three problems with Langer's proposal. First, identical "proportions" and identical "arrangements" do not necessarily occur together. A stretched rubber sheet may retain the adjacencies of its parts—its topology—while changing its proportions. To retain proportions is to retain arrangements, but the converse is not true. Second, just what is an "analogous" arrangement of parts? How much latitude can be allowed before an arrangement is no longer even "analogous"? The word "analogous" is only a synonym for "alike," I suppose. Third, what *kinds* of arrangements are required to be identical? To have "something in common" is not enough, for everything has something in common with anything, if only the fact that the two are both "things." Langer does not discuss this problem, nor do Morris or Ogden and Richards. Goodman, in a characteristic coup de grace, observes dryly (p. 4) that "in many cases neither one of a pair of very like objects represents the other: none of the automobiles off an assembly line is a picture of any of the rest . . . [and] while a painting may represent the Duke of Wellington, the Duke doesn't represent the painting. . . .

Plainly, resemblance in any degree is no sufficient condition for representation."

Another reason why resemblance is not a helpful definition of depiction is that it often smacks of circularity. A picture depicts because it resembles. But how do we know what it resembles? The quick answer is: Oh, we look at it and see what it depicts. With this answer, there is no way to predict the result (the observer's reports) from the basis for the result (the features of the picture) with the idea of resemblance. If likeness is an impression, it cannot also be the basis for the impression.

Peirce and Wittgenstein offered some ideas about a basis for likeness. Peirce noted that either *parts* can be the items that "resemble" or the *relations between parts* can be (1940, p. 107). Echoing this emphasis on relations, Wittgenstein stated that "what constitutes a picture is that its elements are related to one another in a determinate way," representing "things related to one another in the same way" (1961, p. 15). There is some truth here, but it is put so vaguely that truth is ill served, for Goodman's remarks about assembly-line cars and the Duke of Wellington apply again. A new approach is required, one that will help crystallize the vague notions that pictures and referents share something.

Since a picture is an object, it is possible to describe the physical characteristics of the surface that is a picture. But the effort to describe only the picture's surface—its parts and components and relations between parts—may be clumsy and misleading. It may be misleading because adjacent elements on the picture surface may not be depicting adjacent elements in the world, as two adjacent sections of a picture surface may depict a nearby house and its distant background of hills. The point is that it is not simply the distribution of chemicals on a photographic plate, for example, that is significant about a picture. Instead, the significant fact is that these chemicals structure the light coming from them. At this point, it is instructive to consider a curiosity in the history of picturing, an interesting example that helps make the argument clear, by showing how an analysis of daubs and marks and chemicals on a surface may be clumsy compared to an analysis of the light yielded by the surface.

Pictures can be made that seem like distorted representations of objects when looked at head-on—that is, with the line of sight to the center of the picture perpendicular to the surface of the picture. Such pictures can be artfully constructed so that when viewed obliquely (with the line of sight making an acute angle with the surface of the picture) they seem to present an undistorted view of the represented object. Such pictures are called *anamorphics* (Gombrich, 1961, p. 252). One easy way to make an anamorphic picture is to tilt the screen in front of a projection lantern. An anamorphic picture looked at from the *side* yields the same percept as a more usual picture viewed directly in *front*. The arrangement of elements (points or shadows) on an anamorphic picture and on a regular picture may be quite different, but they may result in the same percept.

Any theory that relies on descriptions of the elements and their distribution on a surface is inconvenienced by anamorphics. And where only commonality of features is stressed, the logical problem arises that anything shares features with anything else. To muddle matters more, the practical problem arises that pictures are flat, but the depicted scene is not. What can be in common between a flat picture and a scene in depth! It may aid matters if, following the lesson of anamorphics, a start is made on a description incorporating the concept of a point of observation, and the light to that point. That leads into the third theory of the nature of pictures.

Station Points and Pictures

One definition of a picture that might be offered is that a picture is a surface treated so that it yields light to a particular station point, usually on a normal to the picture surface, which could have come from a scene in the real world.

This definition of a picture has the dignity of age; many artists have searched for an illusion of reality with this definition as a philosopher's stone (Gombrich, 1961). For many years an aura of illusion or Magick surrounded this definition. The suggestion of trickery is well shown in a story from Arnheim (1954, p. 97): "An artist was sketching the house of a German peasant while the owner was watching him. As he was drawing the oblique lines of perspective, the peasant protested: 'why do you make my roof so crooked, my house is quite straight!' But when he later saw the picture finished he admitted with surprise: 'Painting is a strange business. Now it is my house, just the way it is!' " The picture and the house have the same optical effects but not the same arrangement of surface elements.

To show the age of the definition we can note that, as far back as 1715, Taylor wrote: "We must consider that a picture painted in its utmost degree of perfection ought to affect the eye of the beholder so that he should not be able to judge whether what he sees is only a few colors laid artificially on a cloth or the very objects there represented, seen through the frame of the picture as though through a window. To produce this effect, it is plain the light ought to come from the picture to the spectator's eye in the very same manner as it would do from the objects themselves." Gombrich (1961, p. 299) manages to trace this concept of a picture as a kind of window back as far as Alberti and Da Vinci.

Some cautions have to be put into the definition. A picture's materials "only reflect some aspect or projection of its subject," and depiction is "always partial and incomplete" (Bernheimer, 1961, p. 137). Some pictures are schematic, revealing only a limited part of their subject. Others provide details that are so complete that a magnifying glass can be used to discover the artist's finer work. But even the most filigreed painting will be missing some things.

A concept to the extent to which the light from a picture is more completely a presentation of the light from its subject is necessary. One formulation was offered by J. J. Gibson (1954) who defined the fidelity of a picture as the extent to which it represented light from a scene. He worked his way to a depiction of fidelity as follows. First he said: "A faithful picture is a delimited physical surface processed in such a way that it reflects or transmits a sheaf of light-rays to a given point which is the same as would be the sheaf of rays from the original to that point." Then he asked when a picture would be a faithful picture, whether there were any rules for making faithful pictures. In fact, as he wrote, "the definition is equivalent to saying that a picture may be considered as a geometrical projection, and that the relation of a picture to its original is given by a polar projection of a three-dimensional solid on a plane."

As Gombrich (1961, p. 97) says of Leonardo, "mathematics was to help him be the true maker." Ultimately, Gibson proposed (1954, p. 8) the fidelity of a picture could be checked as follows: "A sheaf or ray is the 'same as' another when the adjacent order of the points of color in the cross section of one is the same as the adjacent order in the cross section of the other."

Perspective is a powerful tool for depiction, as its use since the Renaissance in the making of paintings plainly shows. Its ready acceptance in non-Western cultures is one of the arguments used to show that it is not merely one among many purely conventional coding procedures (Gombrich, 1972). "Perspective may be a difficult skill, but its basis . . . rests on a simple and incontrovertible fact of experience, the fact that we cannot look around a corner" (Gombrich, 1961, p. 250). Any picture that satisfies the criterion of perspective geometry and Gibson's criterion for fidelity will necessarily generate an optic array that, within the subtended solid angle of the picture at the station point, could have come from the original scene. This perspective theory based on light projection can readily account for anamorphic pictures. In anamorphics, the correct station point is not on a normal to the surface; it is on an oblique to the surface.

Even the most careful critics of exact perspective (like Pirenne, whose ideas will be considered later) do not doubt that, with the eye at the correct station point, perspective is a basis for making a picture. It is one of the best-developed tools in the science of perception and deserves a much fuller treatment than yet given it by psychologists. But just as important as the mathematical tool is an idea about where to apply the mathematics. Gibson's attempt at a definition of fidelity is one step in the direction of a theory of the optics to which geometry can be applied. And that step is a useful place on which to test the definition of pictures as perspectively faithful renderings. A revealing question is, fidelity to what? To what aspects of the environment must depictions be faithful? Points? Objects? Whole scenes?

Gibson rested his analysis, in 1954, on points of color. But what have points of color to do with *outline drawings*? The surface of outline drawings usually consists of white paper with elongated narrow deposits of black pigment that surround areas of white space on the paper. Few black and white drawings are colored in any way like the original scene being pictured.

The deposits of pigment in an outline drawing could be in projective correspondence with the edges of an object—a chair, for instance. Where in the optic array from a chair there occurred the projection of an edge of the chair, there now in the optic array from the drawing is a corresponding projection from the deposit of pigment. The surfaces of the chair, bounded by its edges, project solid angles in the optic array from the chair, to which there correspond solid angles of light in the optic array from the drawing. Yet, unfortunately, on any definition of fidelity relying on Gibson's condition that the adjacent order of the points of color in the cross section of one is the same as the adjacent order in the cross section of the other, the fidelity of the line drawing would be quite low. Uniform white spaces and their projections have little correspondence with the projections of the textured, shadowed surfaces of a chair that has metallic legs and a red-leather seat and a dark, grainy, wooden back. Yet the chair would be recognizable in a line drawing.

A points-of-color definition of fidelity is often very unhelpful. Such a definition might distinguish schematic or pointillistic work from a photograph or an attempt at *trompe l'oeil,* but it would not pick out differences between schematic, casual, outline, and caricature drawings. When the concept of fidelity relies upon point measures, any deviation from identical spectral composition and intensity will be considered unfaithful representation. A careful line drawing and an improperly colored and proportioned painting will then both be considered "unfaithful." Yet though the poor painting may be vague or in error, the line drawing may be an exact depiction of the distribution of the object's surfaces.

What concepts are needed to distinguish a careful line drawing from a slapdash painting? The answer lies perhaps in the terms we use to describe objects and scenes, the terms I used to describe a chair depicted in a drawing—namely, the edges and components of layout. These are features of objects. They are the shapes into which surfaces fall. If we consider these features, we may find that a deceptively simple correction may salvage the concept of fidelity and help us understand outline drawings. The correction can be mentioned here in a few words, and later chapters can fill in the necessary details.

In principle, *the test for fidelity can be applied to each aspect of the object that helps structure the optic array.* The test for fidelity could be applied separately to each feature of the object, as distinguished from each point of the object. The apparent simplicity of this proposal is deceptive, for to define the features of objects is no small task, as later attempts at definitions will show. And the proposal creates as many mysteries as it solves. For example, why should a black line depict an edge of a surface? There are many differences between black lines and the edges of surfaces. Depiction of one by the other is a mystery that may only deepen as this analysis unfolds!

But for now, in principle the proposal offers a possible way round the impasse presented by definitions relying on point-of-color correspondence. The proposal is that the lines in a line drawing, if they are perspective projections of the edges of a chair, are faithful to the edges of the chair. Fidelity to the object as a whole would be checked by verifying that each feature of the chair that was of interest is represented faithfully in the optic array from the picture. One could separately test, for example, the layout of edges and colors and distributions of texture. Perhaps the shadows and highlights might be of interest, too. Or do shadows and highlights seem a little too much? Can a line drawing depict features based on shadows or highlights? Are there more features that should be considered, such as texture? These are the trickier details that can be debated later. For now, to follow the logic of the discussion, it is enough to note the principle that fidelity can be defined in terms of features, whatever they are, rather than in terms of points of color. Rather than try to fill in all the practical details, let us evaluate the core of the definition.

The analysis in terms of points of color was projective, and relied on exact chromatic values and exact adjacency of points of color. The concept of projection has not been rejected in the change to features and their shapes. All I have done is replace "points" with "features." Perhaps in the last resort, the concept of exact projection has to be amended, too. Perhaps it is both too vague and too limited. Perhaps it is adequate for describing some kinds of displays but not for defining pictures in general. That is, the concept of projection may totally fail as a general criterion, even if it is occasionally useful as a tool for making pictures, just as a pencil is useful for making pictures but pencil marks are not the defining criteria of pictures, since not all pictures are made with pencils.

The concept of projection is too vague for precisely the same reason that the "common properties" hypothesis failed. That everything has something in common with anything was a flaw in the common properties formulation of a picture. Similarly, a straight line could be a projection of any of a host of things; it is a perspective projection of too many things for it to be a picture of anything. A single line would need companion lines before it clearly depicted a horizon, or a string or the leg of a chair or whatever. So it is impossible to take one component of a picture, and say that it could be a projection of and thus what it depicts in this case. It is necessary to ask not only what it might depict (what host of things could be depicted by that line) but what it depicts in this particular case. Pictures are not simply individual lines but whole groups of components, and the overall pattern must be considered as much as any one line. Exact projection of one feature onto another, as a defining criterion, is too vague in the sense that it allows too much latitude to any single component. It is the feature in relation to other features that matters, not the single isolated component. So it will be necessary to invoke a concept of specificity, as was done in Chapter Two in order to define optic information. The definition of fidelity will then apply to features, but only to features within patterns, like whole objects or parts of objects or groups of features in the environment. Pictures are specific to whole patterns of the environment, not just to individual features.

A second reason to invoke the concept of specificity is that the concept of exact projection may be too limiting. One of the most effective means of representing some kinds of objects, perhaps any object, is a special kind of picture that is not a geometrically exact projection. A caricature, for instance, is that kind of effective picture that defies the canons of exact projection. Children's drawings, too, are often instantly meaningful, although they break almost every possible rule of geometry. Pirenne in painstaking fashion showed that even simple geometrical figures can be depicted in ways that refuse to conform to the laws of geometry. So a broader concept of projection is necessary, broader than exact projection.

In caricature, at least, departures from projective correspondence are unmistakably present, yet their representational skill is unquestionable, it is so very powerful. In response to studies on caricatures (ones I will discuss in detail later), J. J. Gibson recently (1972) began to formulate another analysis of pictures. Not all of his problems are solved, but he has begun to develop a fourth approach to pictures whose logic deserves serious consideration. The approach begins from the belief that the unvarnished concept of exact projection is inadequate. The crux of this fourth approach is the concept of optic information.

Information and Pictures

In 1954 Gibson was arguing that departures from accurate perspective projection—that is, "distortions"—would be of value only if the observer accepted them as symbolic. Since then he has come to rethink the implications of his theory of perception. "Vision depends on the structure of the optic array," he wrote in 1960, "however this may have been caused." The more he has emphasized optic structure, the more he has demoted the points of color, light energy, and the point-by-point concept of fidelity.

This is merely common sense. A black-line drawing on a white paper, and a white-chalk drawing on a blackboard need not share one common point, measured in terms of reflectance but nevertheless can be obviously of the same subject. Any identities in the optic arrays from the black board and the white paper will be established on a higher order analysis than points. A most difficult question is, what should the level of analysis be? Should it be the *proportions* of, say, the various edges of the object that must be maintained in the picture? But that is the very thing that excludes caricatures, where the nose might be ten times larger than the forehead, rather than twice, as in the original.

What we are looking for is a definition of depiction that would cope with both line drawings and caricatures. The definition must be in terms of variables of structure, and the definition should help us identify which structural variables are relevant. Gibson's newest suggestion is that "A picture is a surface so treated that a delimited optic array to a point of observation is made available that contains the same kind of information that is found in the ambient optic arrays of an ordinary environment" (1971, p. 31).

Gibson's proposal is very general, but at least it meets some criteria for a satisfactory definition, and it avoids the pitfalls of other definitions. It is expressed in terms of information, which is based on the concept of specificity not likeness or commonality, so the problems of common properties posed by defeated definitions do not arise. The differences in optic arrays from different objects are relevant, appropriately enough, in Gibson's theory—indeed, the differences are the foundation of his theory of perception (see Chapter 2, and Gibson and Gibson, 1955). In the theory, information is based on optic structure, not isolated elements, so the patterns formed by features or components are relevant. The definition is in terms of optics, so it offers an ecological basis for pictorial perception and is not merely a circular reference to impressions of similarity, which created difficulties for a definition in terms of likeness. The logic of the definition appears to be sound.

The definition is very general. Can it be spelled out so that it can be used in particular cases? There are two ways to go from here. First, we can ask if the definition has at least some specific testable implications. Second, we can ask whether Gibson can list the informative variables that are supposed to be made available by pictures.

Certainly there are definite testable implications to a definition of pictures phrased in terms of optic information. For one thing, any subject who was accustomed to identifying objects or distances or arrangements of surfaces in the "ordinary environment" should be able to make the same identifications using optic arrays from pictures. Observers should not need to be trained in any pictorial convention. Another prediction is that specific detailed features of the environment that an observer can identify, given an optic array from the actual feature in the environment, should be efficiently depicted in any picture that conveys the same optic structure. For example, outline pictures should be able to depict all of the basic features of the environment that structure the light to the eye. (We can recognize edges of surfaces and distinguish them from variation in the color of a surface. We can tell the difference between highlights and shadows. We respond to differences in texture. Therefore, outline *depiction* of edges of surfaces, pigmentation, highlights and shadows, and arrangements of texture should all be recognizable without any hints or training.) I will compare these predictions with the results of experiments in later chapters.

Besides asking for specific predictions, we could try to bring Gibson's definition down from the clouds of generality. Can we fill in Gibson's general definition? Unfortunately, it is difficult to list the relevant informative optic variables. To do so would require our having precise definitions of optic structures. But the informative shapes and arrangements of solid angles of the optic array are too complex for today's geometry of optics. What is the shape of a solid angle of light that comes from a man? How does it differ from the shape of a solid angle from a tree? As yet, we simply do not know the shapes that men project (the shapes that are in common to the projections of men), the shapes that are distinctive to men and distinguish men from trees. Consequently, Gibson's definition of a picture is "promisory"—it fulfills the general criteria, it is logically sound and it makes definite predictions, but it cannot be fully spelled out in every individual case yet.

At most, Gibson's definition can be used to guide our thinking about pictures, for he can only suggest some properties of light that might be informative. He says, "Information consists of invariants . . . of the structure of an optic array" (1971, p. 31). Technically, an invariant is a property that is constant across a change. An optic invariant is a property that is constant across changes of illumination on the scene, or change of station point, or some rotations of the object. There may be optic invariants even if there are no identical point elements. Optic invariants may be informative about their sources in the ordinary environment, and what is not invariant may reveal the changes in the sources of illumination, like the sun, or changes in the location of the point of observation (Gibson, 1966, p. 264).

How can a picture reveal "an invariant"? Static pictures produce optic arrays that could be "frozen moments" in an ordinary environment. This means pictures can never provide more information than is present in a frozen array, and hence pictures may be ambiguous about properties of the environment that are specified only across arrays. But it is important to note that whatever is invariant across optic arrays is present in the frozen optic array. Provided the observer has had an opportunity to discover what is typically invariant across optic arrays, *he may be "tuned" to those structural variables and so notice then when they are present in a frozen array*, without their invariance having to be demonstrated each time. So one can say with Gibson (1971, p. 31) that a picture "contains the same kind of timeless invariants that a sequence of perspectives contains."

Gibson is emphasizing invariants, variables that remain constant despite some changes. Normally, these changes involve rotation or change of illumination. But even the stretching and bending involved in caricature preserves some relations. Thus, in a caricature of a politician with a large nose, the profile may contain a small convex curve joined to a much larger convex curve. The small curve represents the forehead, the large one the nose. The conjunction of the two involves an exaggeration that preserves size differences, though not to exact scale, and so is informative about the relations (though not the scale) between the nose and the forehead in the original.

A picture presents a frozen, perhaps exaggerated moment in the set of transformations that would reveal invariants. The observer is tuned to the relevant invariants of structure. This argument is close to one made by Bernheimer, who wrote that a depicted scene will be perceived—will "maintain itself as distinct and separate"— only when "the beholder is aware of the existence of various ways, even though none be specifically known, in which its content may be expressed" (1961, p. 147). Bernheimer's claim is mysterious until one realizes that pictures reveal frozen instances of a property that is invariant across different instances—that is, frozen moments taken from the total transformation that shows a property to be invariant. In a metaphor, Bernheimer suggests that "the subject is not contained by a work of art, but pointed out by it as something that has an existence apart" (p. 155). He remarks that "if an interpretant [the observer] is confronted with a likeness . . . he will realize that what he beholds is only one among an indefinite number of other likenesses that could be made of this one theme" (p. 127).

Bernheimer does not say by what means pictures reveal properties that would be evident in other views. But his claims suggest a concept of information supplied by optic structure, present in a frozen moment, invariant across changes in the normal environment.

Bernheimer, a philosopher, describes some of the effects of looking at static pictures. Gibson suggests the kinds of physical things that a picture depends on for its effects. In the last resort, Gibson can suggest only a very general definition. The range and variety of pictures and the complexity of light and its patterns defeats any contemporary attempt to arrive at more than a general definition. Since we cannot be explicit, the attempt to refute the "pictures are conventions" view has not completely succeeded. Today, geometry, optics, and logic cannot completely defeat that view. Can research and experiments? The next chapters review the evidence.

Chapter Four

Deception and
Development of
Picture Perception

*M*an invented pictures and turned them to many ends. By now his invention has as many forms as functions: doodles, cartoons, sketches, paintings, photographs, stained-glass windows. The torrent of images in our culture pours on us from every possible corner, for every possible reason: to propagandize, identify, give pleasure, comfort, and remind. We are amused, puzzled, and informed by pictures. Pictures stimulate imagination; we tell stories around photographs. We use pictures in books to attract the reader's attention, to inform him about the

47

content, to give him an efficient way to recall the content, and to evoke a background of associations about it.

The idea that pictures deserve scientific experimental investigation is very recent; an experimental psychology of pictures is barely under way, and only a few studies provide anchorages in a sea of issues in the psychology of pictures. The issue of this book being the way pictures provide information, that is the principle by which I have selected studies to consider here. By and large, the studies show pictures can be quite accurate with just minimal instructions to the subjects.

The *bête noire* of this chapter is the view—indeed, virulent prejudice—that, somehow, pictures are necessarily conventional, tied to the culture that produces them by strong and quite arbitrary canons of depiction. (I find most of my students hold this view when they first come into my courses.) This explanation emphasizes the choice exercised by cultures and individuals, the variability of picture perception, and the differences between cultures. Later, when some of the complexities of picture perception become more evident, this view will be considered quite favorably; but as a general explanation of picturing, it is sadly misleading. It is discomfited by the ways a perceiver can be deceived with high-fidelity pictures and by evidence from animal and child psychology. It leads to muddled thinking just as often as it enlightens, when evidence from other cultures is debated.

A comprehensive psychology of pictures cannot be written, yet, but in this chapter I will try to describe the studies from which exploration might depart, and later I will briefly summarize the difficulties that remain to perturb the arguments. First, let us take up *trompe l'oeil* (literally, "tricks the eye"), the question of how pictures can come to be deceptively close to the original.

Trompe l'Oeil

There have been times when realism was a criterion for good representation and other times when it was maligned as an attempt to deceive. To make matters more puzzling, there have been still other times when realism was said to be impossible. Realism as a criterion for the value of a work is not important to my argument now, but it is important to be clear on whether pictures can deceive the perceiver into thinking the depicted things are present.

There are many references in antiquity to artists whose work was so astute that the beholder would "almost think he was there." Gombrich (1961) gives this elegant account of an anecdote from Pliny: "Parrhasios trumped Zeuxis, who had painted grapes so deceptively that birds came to peck at them. He invited his rival to his studio to show him his own work, and when Zeuxis eagerly tried to lift the curtain from the panel, he found it was not real but painted, after which he had to concede the palm to Parrhasios who had deceived not only irrational birds but an artist" (p. 206). And Gombrich notes, "the most successful *trompe l'oeil* I have ever seen was on the level of Parrhasios' trick—a painting simulating a broken glass pane in front of a picture" (1961, p. 207).

We may be suspicious of anecdotes, which grow with handling, and we may be as suspicious of commentary, with all the desire for emphatic statement that it is heir to. Arnheim notes it was said of Giotto that he seemed to depict "the thing itself" so well that "many times the visual sense of men was misled . . . believing to be true what was only painted" (1954, p. 116). As Arnheim says, it was probably the difference between Giotto's work and his contemporaries' that invited hyperbole, rather than simply a skill that never departed from optic fidelity to the physical world.

To avoid hyperbole, it is necessary to turn to experiments and well-documented procedures for making tests. Gibson (1960) attempted a contemporary version of the tradition of *trompe l'oeil*. He made a large photomural from a photograph of a long and dimly lit corridor. The photomural was arranged behind a peephole in a screen, and another screen and peephole was arranged at the end of the real corridor. Subjects looked, monocularly, into each peephole and had to judge which peephole looked into the real corridor and which into the photograph. Both the photograph and the corridor subtended the same angle to the eye, and the edges of the photograph were not visible. The structure of the optic array projected by the corridor was replicated in the optic array from the photograph. About a third of the subjects judged the photograph to be the real corridor. Thus, the *trompe l'oeil* experiment seems to be successful even when the pictorial scene is arranged side by side with the original scene.

In Gibson's study, there must have been some basis for judging accurately, for the subjects' reports were not evenly split, a random 50-50 distribution. Only a third were fooled. Perhaps with a full, careful look, all subjects could have judged correctly, since the photomural was purely black and white and so lost some of the subtleties of color and shade that would have been present in the optic array from the real corridor. But an improved picture could be made in which there would be fidelity of color as well as fidelity of intensity of light. With a little technical skill, the range of intensity, which is normally slightly less in a photograph than in the real scene, could be increased and improved. The fact that a good number of subjects were fooled is the important fact, of course; it is only a reasonable supposition that the photograph could be made undetectably different from the original in peephole viewing.

That some subjects did not seem to make use of slight but informative differences is important. It suggests an element of choice in picture perception, a choice over the kind of detail that is to be considered relevant. Thus, there may be an important place for a distinction between what is chosen to be relevant and what is chosen to be irrelevant. This kind of choice is not quite the same as a choice between objects that might be represented, the kind of choice emphasized in the view that pictures are arbitrary conventions. One is a choice over what parts of the picture and its optic array are relevant; the other is a choice over what can be depicted once the relevant parts are selected. The difference in the kinds of choices should be relevant to studies comparing children to adults and to cross-cultural studies, for it may be that cultures are able to tell their members where to look but not what to see when they look there. Thus, the distinctions suggested by Gibson's study must be borne in mind when the cross-cultural studies are raised.

A second study on *trompe l'oeil* reinforces the distinction. Hochberg (1962) made a relief model of a house, with a depth of 2.5 centimeters, all the materials being one color. Then the model was sprayed with paint from an angle which simulated a direction of illumination of variance with the illumination of the room in which the model was viewed. The model was placed in a frame with a thick, black border, and finally it was given a plane, transparent cellophane cover to simulate the plane surface of a picture. Both a flat picture of the model and the model itself were displayed several feet in front of subjects. In spontaneous observation and comments the subjects did not distinguish the two. Both the model and its picture were taken to be flat pictures.

The relief depth of Hochberg's model was large enough to be visible at the viewing distance, yet it was not discerned by the students. Just as Gibson's subjects often did not pick up fine, telling differences between a real corridor and its photograph, so Hochberg's subjects did not pick up real relief depth when the misleading paint, border, and cellophane were present. The relief depth was not effective; misleading context seemed to lessen the possibility that it would be detected. Apparently, the customary context of a picture told the subjects not to look for depth in a cursory glance.

Gibson continued the tradition of *trompe l'oeil,* making a picture seem reality. Hochberg turned the tradition around, finding that real differences were not detected. Both studies show how close an optic array from a picture can be to an optic array from the world in affecting perception. And both studies suggest that observers have to consider what is relevant in an optic array as well as what to do with the relevant components of an optic array.

Both Gibson and Hochberg used photographs to investigate *trompe l'oeil* problems. Photographs are suitable because they accurately replicate shading and coloring, whose absence would be a sure giveaway in any reasonable examination. One would not expect a negative of a photograph or a sketchy painting to fool an observer. Perhaps there are rare exceptions to this rule. As light relief, consider an observation on possible *trompe l'oeil* from a line drawing.

For curiosity I once presented a subject with a line drawing that invited *trompe l'oeil.* It was of a scene with children playing (Fig. 7). On the same page but to one side of the central scene was a line drawing of a pencil, drawn complete with an eraser and a sharp point. The subject was required to add a drawing of a figure in the midst of the children. To his embarrassment, on two occasions the subject, gazing thoughtfully at the space where he was to draw, reached out his hand to pick up the line-drawn pencil!

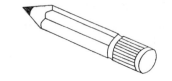

FIGURE 7. A figure like this one was shown together with instructions to add the missing central figure. Some subjects, gazing at the blank central space, have absent-mindedly reached out to pick up the line-drawn pencil.

It is difficult to believe a line drawing could have been deceptively real; the thin, black-ink lines are so unlike the edges of a pencil, the junction of a rubber eraser with its holder, or the contours of wood and paint at the tip of a pencil. But it is equally difficult to believe that the subject's error occurred at some cognitive level divorced from perception—that is, that he might have tried to pick up the *word* "pencil" if it had been there instead of the line drawing. The only reasonable explanation is that a pictured pencil, drawn with lines, may occasionally be taken for the real thing if it is on the periphery of vision.

Even a generous critic may scoff at the idea that an outline can result in *trompe l'oeil*. But even the hardest critic will have to reckon seriously with the Gibson and Hochberg studies. The evidence is clear: pictures can be deceptively lifelike. Pictures are not necessarily arbitrary, unrelated optically to the scenes they represent.

One further note: Schlosberg has shown that the devices used by Gibson and Hochberg enhance the observer's impressions that a depicted scene is more lifelike. As compared to binocular observation, from two station points, monocular observation makes the depiction more "real." The impression is strengthened if one looks through a peephole and cannot see the frame of the picture or move one's head and obtain views from many station points. (Interposing a lens can help, too.) Objects seem more definitely to "stand out" in a more full, three-dimensional space, with Schlosberg's procedures.

Once it is established that pictures can fool the observer, it comes as no surprise to know they can provide information about distances between parts of a scene. Judgments made with pictures are often as accurate as any made while one is directly inspecting the scene. Quite a number of studies taking off from Gibson's study with the photomural emphasize this point.

Accuracy of Pictorial Information

Smith and Smith (1961) arranged a photograph of a room behind a screen and peephole. Behaving even more dramatically than Gibson's subjects, in this study no subject reported under questioning that he realized he was looking at a photograph. The subjects were asked to throw a ball at a target in the room. To the real scene subjects responded with a range from 96 percent (an average underthrow) to 100 percent (on target). To the photograph the throws ranged from 97 to 106 percent (an average overthrow). Thus, accuracy to the photograph was good and comparable to accuracy with the real scene.

Smith (1958) presented Gibson's black-and-white photomural of the corridor, 360 feet long, to subjects who were asked to estimate the number of paces from the viewpoint to specific parts of the pictured scene. Not only could subjects perform accurately on this task, but they were able to estimate the number of paces between places in the scene (and varying the magnification of the scene changed the number of paces appropriately). Afterward, Smith writes, "nearly every subject made some inquiry such as 'I know it isn't real, but how did you do it!' "

Smith and Gruber asked subjects to compare the apparent

length of the real corridor and the apparent length of the depicted corridor. Subjects were able to make these comparisons, although the depicted corridor was slightly and consistently overestimated for unknown reasons. (More importantly, for a theory of projection, when the depiction was magnified, in several steps, at every stage of magnification the subject's judgments followed the magnification almost exactly.) Overall, any errors were "minute," Smith and Gruber note (p. 310).

Smith, Smith, and Hubbard compared judgments of distance in (1) a black and white photograph of a corridor, (2) a line drawing of the corridor with a great deal of detail, (3) a line drawing with less detail, (4) a line drawing with even less detail but with the further parts of the corridor depicted as darkened, and (5) a similar line drawing but without the darkening. In (4) and (5), only the corners of the corridor, the junctions of the walls with the floors and ceiling, and a change in the color of the walls— about one-third up the wall—were depicted, all by lines.

Subjects compared the apparent distance to the end of the corridor in the photograph with the apparent distance to the end of the corridor in the line drawings, saying whether the distances were equal to one another, or one was nine-tenths of the other, and so on. They also compared the apparent width of the corridor in the various pictures. The photographs and the line drawings yielded "equivalent perceptions of distance . . . neither detail nor shading changed the relationship" (p. 673). Geometrical predictions and the judgments obtained from subjects correlated very highly (0.97). According to the researchers, "There is no evidence that depth perceived in perspective line drawings differs from that of photographs" (p. 674). And, as Smith and Gruber found, subjects were "highly sensitive" to magnification of one display compared to another, even though they were not adept at geometry or told anything about the magnification being applied. Smith, Smith, and Hubbard concluded: "Ratio judgments of the depth perceived in line drawings to the depth perceived in photographs can be made easily by naïve observers, with high sensitivity to changes in viewed perspectives of the line drawings" (p. 675).

The Smith studies are unequivocal. There is no doubt that pictures can not only simulate reality, they can also allow accurate judgments of distance that are as accurate as any made in the real scene. The fit of predictions from geometry to the observer's judgments is acute. Different kinds of pictures, all of which provide some of the structure of the optic array from a real scene, corroborate one another nicely. The finding that both many and few details allow comparable judgments is very useful. The finding supports the contention that the fidelity of a picture to a scene can be evaluated separately for each aspect of the represented scene.

The fit of predictions and observers' judgments is rarely perfect. But then, some errors always creep in when subjects pay greater or lesser attention to the task, and there is rarely a perfect fit of geometrical predictions and observers' judgments even when the subjects view a real scene (Vogel and Teghtsoonian).

The Smith, Smith, and Hubbard study is another that calls attention to the need for observers to separate the relevant and the irrelevant. The progressive shading from light to dark toward the far end of the corridor is in principle a distraction. Some mistaken people argue that a brightness gradient is information for distance. But, of course, as distance falls off, so the area projecting light to the eye in a unit of visual angle increases and provides exact compensation. There is no brightness gradient at the eye from a uniformly illuminated slanted surface. Thus, observers must have treated the progressive shading in the picture of the corridor as irrelevant. Apparently they were so adept that the shading was unable to affect their distance judgments.

However, all of the observers were adults, and one wonders whether children would have been as successful. Can children separate the relevant and the irrelevant in depiction spontaneously, or is some kind of helpful training necessary? With this question in mind, let us turn to the evidence on children, some of which is as dramatic as any in psychology, some of which is at least as unequivocal as the Smith studies and the attempts at *trompe l'oeil*.

Children and Depiction

In the last few years there has been a sudden rise in the interest in children's perception of pictures. For a long time the expressive skills of children or their preference for one kind of design or another were the topics that attracted research. But of late the more cognitive questions, the problems facing children as they try to get information about their world, seem to have captured the limelight in psychology. The change is only partly due to fashion or the mood of contemporary psychology. What has been established is remarkable and deserves serious attention.

First, it is now, beyond any tinge of doubt, simply wrong to assert that recognition of pictures requires instruction in a convention of representation. And it is probably wrong to say "it requires practice to see the meanings and the spatial relations in two-dimensional representations and displays" (Stone and Church, 1968, p. 329). The crucial study was conducted by Hochberg and Brooks (1962).

Hochberg and his wife raised their child with restricted exposure to any kind of picture. As far as possible, pictures were removed from the child's vicinity. His parents even removed labels from cans and bottles. Sadly, there were no picture books for him to leaf through. A few decals and an occasional advertising billboard were the only pictorial displays the child encountered. The child had minimal practice in seeing "the meanings and spatial relations in two-dimensional representations and designs."

Exposure and practice were limited. Even more importantly, the child was never trained in labeling pictures. No conventions were, so to speak, forced on him. (The blessings of freedom without the resources to take advantage of being free!) The child was never instructed in associations between words and pictures, never told that pictures represented anything, and was never read a story with illustrations in attendance.

Just before the child was two years old, at a time when he had a reasonably large vocabularly, a test was given. Line drawings, like that shown in Fig. 8, and black and white photographs were set in view, and the child was asked what they were. No photograph was shown before a line drawing of the object was offered, and the child's responses were not corrected. The child labeled almost all the pictures correctly, whether they were photographs, complex line drawings with interior detail (like a doll), or simple outline drawings with minimal interior detail (like a key in outline with only one interior line, a circle, as a hole for a key ring).

FIGURE 8.   An outline drawing that was correctly recognized by an infant who had never been taught the meaning of pictures.

Neither advanced age nor schooling seems to be necessary for picture perception to be successful. Nor is specially high level of inteligence, O'Connor and Hermelin (1961) discovered. They tested 72 subjects with a mean I.Q. of less than 50. An under-50 I.Q. means one's measured I.Q. is in the bottom 1 percent of the population. The subjects were given tasks like picking out from a list of spoken words the names for outline pictures they had just seen. The majority of the subjects were able to perform accurately. And naming pictured objects seemed to be even easier than matching pictures—that is, picking out pictures they had seen before. The contention from Gibson and Bernheimer that subjects deal with the thing depicted, not the particular slant and unique viewpoint or design of the picture, is given support by this study. The subjects found it easier to name the depicted object than to recall a particular display they had recently seen. The object, not the design of the picture, is what subjects notice.

Research on *trompe l'oeil* and perception of distance in pictures both suggest that subjects have to distinguish the relevant and the irrelevant aspects of optic information, before acting on the information. The Hochberg and Brooks study, together with O'Connor and Hermelin's results, make it evident that if any skill at culling relevant information is a necessary part of picture perception, it develops without need of tutoring or intellectual sophistication. It seems reasonable that there should be some development in the skill, however, whether or not it needs tutoring. Pictures may capitalize on ecological optics, and everyday perception of the real world. But pictures are not full theatre; they do not mimic as fully as full-dress play. Pictures are flat; they are on surfaces. The perceiver has to unglue the information for the depicted scene from the information for the flat surface, and yet hold both in mind so he does not mistake depiction for reality. Surely, one would think, there is a skill here that cannot be full grown at birth. Over the last decade a number of studies have turned on this exact point.

Bower (1964) tested for transfer of a response from a real cube to a full-color slide of a cube, in infants a few months old. He trained the infants to respond to a solid real cube and found some transfer of the response to other cubes at different distances or other cubes of different sizes than the original. The infants responded very little, if at all, to the full-color slide. The real cube presents binocular information and information across time (as the infant moves its head) for depth and solidity. The slide gives the same colors, and the frozen array that comes to one eye. But across two eyes, or across time, the slide presents information for flatness. The information for flatness seemed to be critical—to be relevant—to the infants. Thus, pictorial information does not seem to dictate recognition in infants; that is, it is irrelevant.

A number of studies using pictures attempt to show that infants are fascinated by human faces. One interpretation of these studies—contrary to Bower's work—would be that the infants understand depicted faces. But Bower's finding that flat pictures do not seem to be recognized by infants is not necessarily contradicted by these studies using depicted faces. It could be the amount of detail or the symmetry of the faces, rather than recognition, that accounts for most of the infants' interest. Hagen (1972) says, in a summary of this research on pictured faces, "it is, at present, impossible to distinguish the meaning behind these responses. Even (the rare) attempts to sort out confounding leave much room for various interpretations" (p. 38). Where investigators claimed that "faceness," and not "degree of complexity" (or some comparable physical, nonsocial variable) was the important factor, Hagen has been able to point out alternative explanations and confounding variables.

To repeat: Bower's study suggests that very young infants are controlled by kinetic or binocular information, and the pictorial information originating from a flat surface is treated as largely irrelevant.

Bower (1966) continued his line of research by training two-month-old infants to respond to a wire triangle partly obscured by an iron bar. Then he presented simply a wire triangle. Infants transferred their response to the triangle when it was completely visible. (They transferred much less to a triangle that was incomplete —that is, that had breaks in its outline that became visible only when the bar was removed.) When Bower repeated the experiment, using slides, the infants had no preference for one test figure over another. Presumably, when the bar and wire triangle were real and not pictured, the infants were able to respond to the progressive occlusion and reappearance of the wire behind the bar. Slight head movements or binocular vision allow occlusion and reappearance. Bower notes "the infant's performance appeared to depend not on static retinal cues but rather on the information contained in variables, such as motion parallax, that are available to a mobile organism viewing a three-dimensional array" (p. 90). Bower's data suggest that early in life static pictures on flat surfaces are seen as mere patches of flat color.

Another Bower study (1971) reaffirms the importance of binocular information in infants and their indifference to pictorial information. He found that infants will reach for an object if it is pictured so that there is appropriate binocular information present. In this study, one picture was presented to one eye, another picture was presented to the other eye. The pictures formed the kind of pairs that correspond to the frozen optic arrays at two adjacent points of observation. Bower's infants reached for the object and cried in distress when there was nothing to grasp. Of course, when the object was present, they grasped it successfully and did not cry. And when only one picture was given, they did not reach. So only binocular vision using paired pictures induced perception of the object, and the infants even thought the object was real, something to be grasped.

Yonas and Hagen (1971) corroborate some of Bower's findings with older children (three to four and seven to eight years old) and adults (college students). The subjects had to judge the size of objects either when viewing through a peephole that restricted vision to one station point or when viewing through a window where both binocular and head-motion information were available.

The subjects were essentially perfect, if binocular and head-motion information was available, even when the objects projected exactly the same angle to the station point. (If the angles projected by the larger objects were *smaller* than the angles projected by the smaller objects, the younger subjects made some mistakes in the wrong direction, about a third of the time.) When subjects viewed through a peephole, losing binocular and head-motion information, nearly all of the three-year-olds judged according to visual angle. It seems that binocular and head-motion information is important and helps to overrule misleading impressions of size given by smaller visual angles.

Then Yonas and Hagen replaced a real alley and real objects with *slides* of the alley and the objects. The adults were unaffected, even when motion parallax and binocular information were present, offering clear information for the flatness of the real layout. But the seven-year-olds "moved away from responding to the (apparent) depth within the slide" when head motion was allowed to reveal information for the flatness of the screen.

Bower finds two-month-olds to be dominated by motion-carried information. Yonas and Hagen find even seven-year-olds to be affected by it when viewing a slide. But adults, according to Yonas and Hagen, are able to discount the conflicting binocular and kinetic information that differs from pictorial information. In Yonas and Hagen's terms, "What changes from age three to adulthood is the magnitude of . . . differences that can be handled by the perceptual system" (p. 8), for seven-year-olds were not impressed by both small, "misleading" visual angles from large objects and also were less impressed by kinetic information than were the youngest subjects. And the adults were even less affected than the seven-year-olds by conflicting information. Bower and Yonas and Hagen show that, the younger the subjects, the more important kinetic information is relative to static information, at least so far as size judgments are concerned.

Adults seem more able than children to deal with conflicts between pictorial information and the flat surface of the picture. An unusual type of picture employed by Elkind (1970) admirably shows up the skill that allows adults to separate the relevant from the irrelevant where pictures are concerned. Elkind used pictures

where many items on the picture are at once a part of the large configuration, like a bicycle or a palm tree, and also complete objects
in their own right, like carrots or bananas (Fig. 9). Elkind would
show, for example, a "car" made of "vegetables." Young subjects
have considerable difficulty saying that they see an X made up of
Ys. They tend to report the X or the Ys, not both. Slightly more advanced subjects report both but seem unable to report both the X
and the Ys at the same time. Adults report both the X and the Ys
and the relation between them. It seems as though either the configuration or its parts have to be handled separately or confusion
arises, for young subjects. Adults handle both together or separately
at will.

FIGURE 9.   A drawing where the parts depict objects, and the whole
configuration is another object. Young children seem to have difficulty with this kind of figure.

Elkind's study shows a fascinating problem created by conflict between the elements of a picture and the totality depicted,
just as Bower reveals the difficulties posed by the contradictions between the flat surface and the depth shown in the picture. Another

kind of conflict, involving detecting the relevant elements and their overall configuration, can be provided by deleting elements. Erasing parts of a figure produces bare patches. Which patches were relevant at the start and which are present only because something has been removed? In general, the perceiver has to see what is depicted despite missing elements. Hypotheses about the perceptual skills necessary to cope with missing elements will be considered later. For now, let us simply note how the skills develop.

A series of studies by Gollin (1960, 1961) indicate that children do less well than adults in this kind of identification problem. Gollin made a series of outline drawings and gradually erased segments of line, until bare hints of the original configuration were present. The drawings depicted familiar objects such as a car or a dog. Children needed much more outline than adults to recognize the objects, and the amount of outline necessary decreased gradually from the youngest subject (five years old) to the adults.

To deal with Elkind's drawings, one must separate the parts from the whole configuration. In Gollin's studies, one must detect the overall configuration even though some relevant parts are missing. Gollin's research suggests that making accurate identifications is more difficult for children, if the displays are impoverished. This is not to say that children are incapable of seeing many configurations or depictions in impoverished displays, or vaguely drawn sketches, or even random designs. Children may be more variable than adults. Or they may be content with a first guess that only uses some of the elements of the picture.

Parents and teachers frequently remark that their children can see things in a picture that an adult would never pick out without hints. A mere blob with a tail can be a cow, for a child. A casual stroke of paint becomes a snake. From a swath of disjointed forms the child may pick out one corner, and call it a flying witch. The little that can be a picture to a preschooler is amazing. Therefore, what Gollin shows is that more and more detail is necessary to ensure that children will be consistent, rather than be variable or be content with a response using only part of the picture. It would be wrong to interpret Gollin's research as showing that a picture must be very detailed if a child is to see it as a picture of something. Children will see a picture in a scribble, but different children wll select different things, our everyday experience suggests. Presumably, with age, selectivity becomes more skilled (Mackworth and Bruner, 1970), more attuned to the requirements of puzzles, and more capable of using all of the elements systematically.

The research literature on children and picture perception makes a number of points. First, training is not necessary for depiction to be meaningful, even with such abstract pictures as line drawings, though for the sake of consistency the pictures should be highly faithful to their objects. Hochberg's drawings were reasonably faithful to their objects—complete outlines were always given and some internal detail, too. Second, there is a skill in picture perception that involves separating the relevant from the irrelevant and, ultimately, making use of the total set of elements on the picture surface and their configuration. Training may assist the development of pictorial skills, but it is not necessary to train children or even provide much experience with pictures in order for pictorial skills to emerge.

One final point: After children note objects in a picture, they seem to be able to relocate them spontaneously in their next exposure to the picture. Children are not completely fickle in choosing what to see; they do not pay scant regard to one feature one time and another feature another time. As most parents have found, children enjoy seeing and recognizing the same pictures again and again. In a useful test of the consistency of children's perceptions, Hoffman (1971) presented groups of children as young as three and five years old with 100 pictures and later tested them for recognition. All the pictures were in color, and none had a single dominant object. Each picture had as much diversity of line and color as possible. No inherently attention-grabbing devices like letters or numbers were displayed, nor were people shown in the pictures. Having seen 100 pictures, the children were asked to select from 20 pairs of pictures any member of the pair that had been shown previously. Even the three-year-olds selected 75 percent correctly, and the five-year-olds scored 82 percent. The diversity of the content in individual pictures did not confuse the subjects. Often the same features were noticed in both presentations of the pictures. My own informal observations of two-year-olds support Hoffman's findings. Children can recognize their own line drawings and say, for example, "that's a pear," even though the shaky outline of a pear is all but buried in a mass of lines.

An interesting theory has been offered by Sakuichi Nakagawa (personal communication 1972) about the development of children's perceptions. He argues that children begin as four-dimensional perceivers. Children register the "events" of their environment, rather than all the static "appearances" of objects. Later they become three-dimensional perceivers, detecting the shapes of objects. Still later they become capable of two-dimensional perception, capable of registering flat shapes or information provided by marks on flat surfaces. This Japanese view developed quite independently of Bower's work. Yet there is a fascinating parallel between Bower's findings and Nakagawa's theory. The crowning touch is that Bower finds that very young infants will not accept a static object as being equivalent to the same object in motion. An infant following a moving object with his eyes will not continue to look at the object when it comes to rest. Instead, he will continue his tracking motion briefly after the object stops, and then look around, for all the world as though he were trying to find a missing object. The stationary object is not "recognized," Bower speculates, as the heir to the moving object (Bower, 1971).

Nakagawa's ideas together with Bower's research suggest a three-step sequence: first, the young infant registers objects in motion and fails to connect a stationary object with the same object in motion. Second, the child recognizes objects that are static, like Bower's cubes, but not when depicted. Third, the infant, in a steadily maturing development of a capacity to recognize the same object in many guises, comes to recognize pictorial information, static information, and motion-carried information as being equivalent.

General theories have a way of being vague and consequently difficult to test. They also have a way of meeting a slow death in the hands of experimental fact. For good reasons, therefore, the Nakagawa theory is offered at the end of my description of experiments. The best spirit in which to take the theory, at this point, is that it is fascinating speculation, a conceivable and imaginative interpretation of the facts, a theory that contrasts with the alternative theory that children have to be taught, piecemeal, a set of pictorial conventions.

Chapter Five

Picture Perception
Across Cultures
and Species

"The picture, particularly one printed on paper," according to Biesheuvel (1949), "is a highly conventional symbol, which the child reared in Western cultures has learned to interpret" (p. 98), and the orthodoxy still holds that unsophisticated subjects are puzzled by even clear photographs. "A Bush Negro woman," Herskovits wrote (1948), "turned a photograph this way and that, in attempting to make sense out of the shadings of grey on the piece of paper she held" (p. 381). Some observers say that nonpictorial peoples find pictures mere daubs. "The natives are frequently quite incapable of seeing pictures at first, and

65

wonder what the smudge is here for" (Kidd, 1904, p. 87). The conclusion is "one can regard the photograph as we use it as an arbitrary linguistic convention not shared by all peoples" (Segall, Campbell, and Herskovits, 1966, p. 33).

Cross-Cultural Research on Pictures

Over the last ten years, the informal observations of anthropologists and essayists have been supplemented by powerful research studies, some of which support the view that untrained subjects are puzzled by "our sophisticated pictures," but other research has begun to challenge this orthodoxy. These arguments and counterarguments have to be examined closely if the consistent threads are to be seen.

Pitfalls in Cross-Cultural Research

Let us begin with some cautionary comments. In many cases, researchers have begun with faulty preconceptions, likely to hinder their considering possible explanations for their findings and likely to prevent their exhaustively checking the intent behind a subject's comments. For example, Segall, Campbell, and Herskovits propose that the "small size" of objects in a sketch or photograph shows that pictures (including photographs) are conventional in nature. (In Goodman's ready phrase, there's nothing like a photograph for turning a mountain into a molehill.) The reasoning is faulty here.

There is no "small object" in a photograph, merely a particular arrangement of pigment. Rather, there is information in the optic array for an object, and information for the size of the object, relative to its surroundings, is also in the optic array, not on the surface of the photograph. Does the phrase "small size" refer to the small angle subtended by the depicted object? If so, the debate is sheer nonsense, for the subtended angle of the real object can be varied just as much as the angle subtended by the represented object. In sum, *photographs do not contain small objects.*

Hudson (1967) asked some Africans to draw an object— just one object—on a sheet of paper. There were enormous variations in the size of the drawing on the sheet. He concludes that the sizes were unimportant to the artists, which seems reasonable. But then he describes the Africans as not playing by our rules, for "in Western pictures we use size as a means for indicating distance" (p. 97). The thing is, *we actually use relative size, not absolute size.* Only when we compare the depicted object with other objects in the same scene can we know its size. Hudson's conclusion could only have been drawn had he asked the Africans to draw a scene with many objects. The notion of size seems to confuse experimenters about as much as any conceivable subject.

Mundy-Castle (1966) reasoned that drawings incorporating perspective would be difficult for Ghanaian children to recognize, for perspective "is a highly abstract concept" (p. 122). But "being human" is similarly highly abstract, and the children easily recognized men in the drawings. The abstractness of a concept bears almost no relation to its use by children. "Toy" is abstract, yet it is one of the first words spoken. The same goes for words like "something" and "nothing" and "all gone." Also drawings using perspective conform to the laws of light, and so should be easier to recognize than drawings violating the laws. Finally, subjects were asked to recognize objects and their arrangement, not describe the laws of light or perspective. Simple recognition does not depend on "abstract understanding," any more than seeing a stone falling depends on understanding the laws of gravity. Mundy-Castle's reasoning seems confused.

The fact remains that anthropologists have noticed many people being puzzled by photographs. Perhaps the reason is simpler than anthropologists think. Photographs are clearly special objects. Would not anyone meeting a photograph for the first time be puzzled, not know quite what to say, but certainly deny that it was, physically, the represented object? How easy it would be for an experimenter, especially if his knowledge of the native language was less than perfect, to interpret inquisitive puzzlement as an inability to take information from pictures. It is very sure that "primitive" peoples show great curiosity over artifacts of our society—just as we show curiosity over their artifacts! Our pictures, print, jewelry, even our illusions fascinate other cultures—not because the subjects find them totally incomprehensible, but because they have a pointed, well-controlled, systematic curiosity. Consider River's (1904) description of the interest the Todas, of the Indian subcontinent, showed in his tricks, notably his illusions:

"Two curved pieces of cardboard of the same size look very different when placed side by side. Many men came to me especially to see this illusion, and they experimented with the pieces of cardboard as intelligently as any European could have done. They tried the effect of placing the cards suddenly and gradually; they tried placing them with their shorter sides in opposition and noted that the cards then appeared of the same size and similarly they placed the cards in every variety of position relative to one another, noting when the illusion was and was not present. . . . Two old men . . . after much experimenting and deliberation . . . gave me the correct explanation, *viz.*, that the short side of one appears shorter than it really is because it is next to the longer side of the other."

Puzzlement and experimenting need not indicate complete lack of understanding. The Todas knew a "trick" when they saw one. It is even possible to make observers who are quite adept with pictures show curiosity and to explore them, to "wonder" as Kidd put it, about photographs. To illustrate this point, let me describe a minor demonstration. I had an unusual photograph taken—the back of someone's head—and placed in an unusual place, the glass part of a partition of a room. The partitions made small cubicles, in which teachers kept office hours. The photograph was visible through the glass wall, and as students approached the cubicle, often their attention was caught by the photograph. Time and again students would first look at the photograph through the glass wall and then crane around the wall to look at the other side of the photograph. They would explain sheepishly that they wanted to see if there was a face on the other side of the photograph! The students were by no means from some isolated Patagonian tribe—they were from New York.

To be puzzled by a picture is not to think that the picture is merely daubs on a surface. Indeed, mere daubs on a surface would hardly puzzle anyone. Daubs hardly invite the viewer to experiment, turning the picture this way and that. The whole game is given way, not in the anthropologists' interpretation of curiosity, but in their footnotes and asides. (There is nothing like a forgotten footnote to discomfit a major conclusion.) Kidd reports "Some see a picture instantly . . . when they see it represents something they are very excited" (p. 88). And Herskovits, in one revealing remark (p. 381), notes "when the details of the photograph were pointed out (to the interested Bush woman) she was able to perceive the subject." Neither Kidd's nor Herskovits's informants needed to be trained in any convention, it seems. It was not as though they were learning a foreign language.

The observation that pictures puzzle people is, at best, open to many interpretations. But casual observations suggest training in a convention is not necessary for comprehension. Let us turn to more controlled studies to see whether they tell us more than do the anecdotes of anthropologists.

Systematic Cross-Cultural Studies

Nadel (1937), in a careful study, showed that Nigerian peoples, with very different kinds of cultures, had little difficulty with photographs. His Yoruba subjects enjoyed a culture that was rich in the use of wooden images and hand-made pictures. The Nube's art was "imageless" in the sense that it was decorative and ornamental, oriented toward design and not depiction. (The Yoruba and Nube lived in adjoining regions with comparable climatic and geographical conditions.) So far as identification of men and animals in photographs was concerned, the people gave like results. Even a photograph of a bush fire, which was dark and indistinct, says Nadel, gave no trouble. Where the people differed was in terms of interpretative comments—for example, how the subject might have come to be where he was shown to be, or what he might be intending to do.

In terms of identification of objects, Nadel's results suggest, widely different cultures recognize pictures in common ways. Only when discussion of the scene or stories about the scene are required will different cultural backgrounds matter. Hudson, in a thoughtful review (1967), notes that some African people tend to interpret a crowd scene such as Fig. 10 as showing people fighting, whereas other African people may see the same scene as part of a dance. Frozen postures tend to be ambiguous, of course, and the viewer's

FIGURE 10.   A crowd scene. Are the people fighting or dancing?
Some cultures have rules that forbid men to dance with men. Other
cultures do not, and these cultural differences could modify general
interpretations of the scene, although there would be wide agree-
ment that the forms in the display all represent people.

culture can be expected to predispose him toward one imaginative
story rather than another.

The tester may ask for, first, identification of the objects displayed; second, their posture; third, the event suggested by the posture; and, finally, the significance of the event. Replies may be uniform at first, then more diverse, and finally a jungle of cultural differences. Identification tasks are like asking the informant to repeat
a word; interpretation is more like free association. European children may interpret a distorted picture of an elephant as a dead elephant, while Africans may describe the same picture as an imaginative depiction of "a dangerous elephant . . . jumping wildly about"
(Hudson, 1967, p. 97). But both kinds of children recognize that
the picture shows an unusual elephant. Sometimes trailing lines, in a
depiction of the head of an animal, for example, might be considered evidence of injury, for the rest of the body is missing (this
comment was offered by African laborers in one of Hudson's studies);
sometimes absence of parts is not in any way significant, even in a
solid model of an animal (to two-and-a-half-year-old African children in French Guinea, discussed by Nissen, Machover, and
Kinder, 1935). Asking for interpretation is asking for cultural
diversity. Not so with recognition.

When a complete depiction of the whole object is shown, or when the object is of a familiar species, or when it is a familiar general type, untrained subjects usually make accurate identifications. Deregowski (1968a), in remote rural Zambia among people with little graphic art, had adult and child (twelve years old) subjects match photographs of toy animals with an array of solid toy animals. Adults showed some difficulty with unfamiliar animals, but this was the only combination of subjects and materials that proved troublesome. Children never had any difficulty, and all groups identified photographs of familiar animals.

Even if photographs were foolproof as representations, effective even for the most unschooled, one might still wonder if line drawings raise special difficulty. Outline depiction leaves out so much and asks us to accept a thin strip of black ink as a corner of, say, a room. Surely we have to be taught about outline drawing.

Hudson (1960) used line drawings like those in Fig. 11 to test many different groups of subjects in South Africa. Some of his subjects were white, some were black, some were illiterate, some educated or attending school. He found that the animals and humans in the pictures *were all fairly consistently identified by all subjects,* in all of his various groups. No subject ever called the outlined man an elephant, and no subject ever called the outlined elephant a man.

Mundy-Castle (1966) repeated Hudson's study with Ghanaians five to ten years old. Like Hudson he did not find any misidentifications of the man. Occasionally a tree was misidentified as flowers, a hand, or a plantain, none of which seem very far from the mark. An elephant was occasionally called a pig or a goat or some other animal, but never a man. A deer was often called a goat or a cow or a horse, which Mundy-Castle thinks is reasonable, for the deer resembles Ghanaian goats and sheep, and deer are rare in Ghana.

Beside the animal and human objects, there were in some drawings occasional sketchy lines, to depict a hill, if curved, or the horizon, if flat, and a pair of converging lines were sometimes present to represent a road. Hudson (1960) wanted to know whether perspective cues, like the convergence of the lines intended as the edges of a road, would be meaningful to his subjects. Many of his white subjects took the lines to be a road, many of his black subjects

FIGURE 11. A line drawing similar to ones used to investigate picture perception in Africa.

took the lines to be spears or a hole. (He reported these details in his 1967 paper.) Since the drawings were sketchy and ambiguous, the question of the meaning of perspective is not fairly tackled by Hudson's study. At least each of the referents mentioned by the black subjects seems quite valid to Western eyes, when the referent is mentioned. The important fact to note is that the lines were not meaningless daubs.

In Mundy-Castle's study, the same kind of "misidentifications" occurred; the road, for example, would be called a river or a rope. The single line for the horizon, the two lines for the road, and the two or three lines for the hill were often misidentified. Given so much ambiguity, it is difficult to be sure whether perspective drawing is meaningless to the subjects, or whether the drawings were simply so sketchy and ambiguous that perspective was rarely in question. One of Deregowski's studies suffered a similar drawback. In this study (reported by Heron, 1968) a road was depicted, by two lines, running between native houses. Even though eighty Zambian school children identified the road correctly, none seemed influenced by the "perspective" provided by the road when judging the size of the houses. In Heron's phrase, the cue was "weak." In a more elaborate drawing, perspective might be more effective.

Hudson also tried to discover whether "overlap" or "familiar size" cues aided some groups but not others in pictorial perception. Both overlap and familiar size cues are often only weak influences on adult perceivers in Western culture (Hochberg, 1964; Kennedy and Brust, 1972). It is not surprising that many of Hudson's subjects seemed to base their replies to his question on logical argument, avoiding relying on weak perceptual cues. For example, some subjects argued that a man would not attack an elephant with a spear, so if the man in a picture was throwing a spear, it must be at the antelope, not the elephant in the picture. Some subjects told Hudson, flatly, that the pictures were ambiguous. If he wanted to question them about the pictures, the subjects said, he should tell them which view they should take.

I tested Hudson's drawings, informally, on students in my classes at Harvard. Like Hudson's African informants, my students said the drawing were ambiguous. Thus, the drawings are bait for cultural diversity and deliberate interpretation rather than spontaneous pictorial perception. Factors like one's belief about hunters and animals enter into replies to Hudson's questions. Presumably, too, such factors as general familiarity with testing procedures would be important. Some subjects know what to do about beliefs ancillary to the pictures, others do not.

Hudson did not discuss the sophistication of his subjects with tests. He did not say whether his subjects were all equally at ease. But surely when a white man pulls a black laborer away from his daily work and sits down in an office with the laborer, and begins to show the laborer little pictures, the laborer begins to feel a little anxious. Especially when the setting is South Africa, the laborer must be uncomfortable. To make matters worse, the white man waits unhelpfully through long periods without deigning to assist the laborer in answering the odd questions the white man is asking. Hudson reports that at times the response was given by the subject after a lag of one hour! What fears were in the laborers' minds we can only guess at. Any skills the laborers displayed, under this kind of treatment, can only be taken to the lowest estimates of their abilities. There is no responsible way in which the probably fearful black laborers' performance can be compared with the performance of white children tested in the familiar, comfortable atmosphere of their own schools.

Deregowski reported that some of his subjects expected job opportunities to hinge on the result of his little tests. How can one expect subjects to behave calmly, at their best, when they are apprehensive (and possibly incredulous) at the kinds of questions being asked?

An intelligent tack was taken by Dennis, who had his tests given by a student who came from the people being tested. In Dennis's study the subjects were asked to make line drawings. The art of the region was decorative rather than depictive. The people were Bedouin tribesmen, nomads to whom any form of graphic activity is alien. The forms of local art were typically simple and rare. Occasional contact with foreigners could provide some exposure to representations, Dennis notes, on coins, bills, and can labels, for example. But exposure to pictures was not an everyday, continual process, and recognition of pictures was not necessary for the normal business of the day.

Dennis asked the subjects to make drawings, which is somewhat unfortunate. Even the worst artist may still be able to identify a picture. But at least the test is conservative, for whatever ability is shown we know is the least the people can do. The tribesmen made their drawings with pencil on paper. They drew human figures, on request, without demur or difficulty, for the most part. They did not seem to think the whole idea was meaningless. Some of the drawings were first made in outline, and then filled in by the subjects. Some subjects left the outlines and did not fill in the inside space. Some subjects would end up with a thick line for a leg, and others would have two thin lines, one for each side of the leg. Some of the tribesmen accepted single lines as depictions of cylindrical objects and others used two parallel lines to depict the boundaries of cylindrical objects. In short, the Bedouins used outlines just as we would.

Even in Western communities there are people with widely different backgrounds and experience, and cross-cultural research can be attempted close to home. Elkind (1970) studied the abilities of preschool and school-starting children from economically poor homes in the United States to see if the rarity of pictures in the homes adversely affected the children's abilities. With poor rural

Sioux children Elkind found an initial unwillingness to cooperate with the experimenter—which an insensitive experimenter could easily have recorded as a "lack of pictorial skills." When Elkind pushed and chided the children a little, they performed as well as children from homes rich in pictures. The same held true for American black children from poor urban homes.

Styles of Representation

One important study compared drawings based on naturalistic optics and its perspective with drawings using a convention common in the art of the region. It is reasonable to suppose that subjects would be best able to get information from a picture that uses familiar conventions. But the facts are otherwise. Deregowski (1970) asked some subjects from a Zambian culture which drawings they preferred as depictions of a set of models. Other subjects from the same culture were asked to pick out the models depicted in various drawings. Some of the drawings were "in perspective," following the canons of geometric optics. Other drawings (Fig. 12, for example), followed the style of the region, where both side views and front views would be included, Picasso-like, in one drawing; Deregowski calls this style "split representation."

FIGURE 12.   A drawing of an elephant in split-representation style.

The subjects preferred drawings in the familiar style overwhelmingly (which suggests they were not overawed by the tester, for they might have chosen the "foreign" style to appease the foreigner). But the perspective drawings were more effective in helping the subjects pick out the model that was depicted. In Deregowski's words: "The preferred drawings are in fact worse than [perspective] drawings in conveying to the subjects what the depicted object actually looks like" (p. 24).

Deregowski's study stands alone: It isolates the efficiency of one mode of drawing from preference shown for various modes of depiction. More studies are needed to bolster Deregowski's findings. It would be surprising to find that most nonperspective styles are decorative rather than communicative, but that is the implication of Deregowski's results.

Deregowski's study also warns us against facile interpretations of drawing practices. Hudson, for example, proposed that the "unacculturated black man" who draws both side and front views in one drawing is drawing something phylogenetically and ontogenetically primitive. Side and front views typify cave art, children's art, and African art. Hudson does not directly say the African is at a childish, primitive stage of development, but the implication is there in the loaded term "unacculturated." Hudson says the unacculturated man draws what he knows and not what he sees. Would Hudson argue that one Bedouin thinks of a leg as a black patch of graphite, whereas another Bedouin thinks of it as two lines? Or would he argue that Picasso is unacculturated because he favors the split-representation style? Interpretations of drawings are touchy propositions, not to be accepted unguardedly. Deregowski helps us clarify the possibility that many practices are preferences unrelated to efficient depiction, and what one "knows" rather than what one "sees."

In another study, Deregowski (1968b) found that many Zambian subjects who misperceived by Hudson's criteria on Hudson's tests perceived more accurately on other tests. By Hudson's criteria, some subjects were failing to attend to depth cues such as perspective overlap and familiar-size cues in Hudson's drawings. But when given other sketches, brief ones of merely a few lines, the subjects would build three-dimensional objects if asked to construct the depicted objects. Cues for depth seem to be meaningful to subjects, even if this ability was not shown on Hudson's test. Page (1970) confirms Deregowski's results. If these drawings used by Hudson are indeed ambiguous, and subjects can use the cues in other situations, then problems with preference dog any attempt by Hudson to interpret his results.

Most studies using outline drawings require subjects to match lines with wires or cylinders or edges of objects. In a provocative break with tradition, Shapiro (1960) asked illiterate Rhodesian Africans to copy colored designs, using only pencil and paper. The subjects were confronted by a design on a flat surface, with areas distinguished only by color. The subjects had difficulty at times reproducing the structured designs Shapiro had concocted, which need not surprise us since the subjects were unfamiliar with tests of this kind. The intriguing result was that the subjects often attempted to *depict* the designs rather than to *reproduce* them. Instead of producing a checkerboard of areas of solid, filled-in pigment, the subjects often preferred to use a quick, efficient way of representing the test pattern, by depicting boundaries with lines. The designs were *depicted* in the sense that contours between areas of pigment were portrayed in outline, without trying to use the pencil like a brush, filling in the areas demarcated by outlines (Fig. 13). The results suggest that boundaries between areas of color can be depicted by line, just as edges of objects can be depicted by line, without need of training in a convention.

To close this review, it is worth noticing, in passing, that

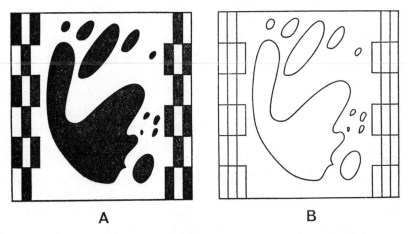

A   B

FIGURE 13. Reproducing design A in a line drawing like B involves using lines as representations of borders between solid patches of color.

Dawson (1967), as part of an enormous research effort in West Africa, tried to teach subjects who misperceived Hudson's drawings (by Hudson's criteria) to improve their scores on Hudson's test. Dawson did everything one could possibly ask for in an elementary course in practical drawing. He explained about depth cues. He had subjects draw on a window lines to depict the scenery visible through the window. He had the subjects interpret their drawings. He had them transfer their drawings to paper and make fresh drawings without first drawing on the window. He familiarized them with elaborate spatial forms and a textbook on perspective, using illustrations of the forms. Almost no one in technological societies receives such thoughtful instructions! Not surprisingly, subjects' scores on Hudson's tests improved dramatically.

Unfortunately, one cannot tell why the scores improved. Did the subjects become more at ease with Dawson? Did they discover the rules of the game called "testing subjects"? Was the improvement due to one part of the training program, or was all of it necessary? That Dawson did not answer these questions is no fault of his—they were not his concern—but it will require a great deal more work to find the answers. For our purposes here, Dawson's main contribution was in demonstrating the dramatic change produced by a short training course. What the change is, Dawson can leave for others to determine.

Summary. Let me try to summarize the cross-cultural research on pictures. There is no clear consensus among psychologists about the results of cross-cultural research in picture perception. Some go so far as to call their subjects unacculturated, and they stigmatize the level of perceptual skill shown as phylogenetically "primitive." Others point out that some picture-making practices are a result of a pleasure and preference; they suggest that aesthetics is as valid as communication efficiency in picture making. Some treat puzzled looks as evidence of ignorance. Some work hard to find out what lies behind disinterest in being tested by alien experimenters. Over the research there still, today, hangs a pall of confused ideas about the very devices that are being investigated. And a thoughtful reader must be disturbed by the lack of concern over the attitude the subjects may have to being tested.

Anyone who hears that Hochberg's two-year-old child

named drawn and photographed objects, without trouble or training, must be suspicious of claims that "primitives" see pictures as meaningless daubs. The fact is that in all the studies most subjects identified most of the depicted objects. What the depicted animals and men seem to be doing is another story; when subjects have to say where the objects are in relation to one another, and what the objects are doing to one another, cultural differences boil up. Wild stories and rationalizations are spun when subjects are asked to do more than identify the objects in pictures. The common core to picture perception—across poor Americans, nomadic Bedouins, South African laborers, and well-schooled children—seems to be recognition of objects. People seem to recognize objects in colored or black and white photographs and in line drawings without trouble. For efficiency, one study suggests, the drawings should be in conformity to geometric laws of light.

As a supportive coda, a study on trained draftsmen in Western technological culture deserves mention. Deregowski (1970, p. 24) quotes a study by Spencer as follows: "Significantly longer time is taken in performing an assembly in accordance with instructions provided by a third-angle projection drawing [the split representation style] than when the instructions are provided by representational [perspective] drawings, in spite of the fact that the former constitutes the standard way of communication which the draftsmen are specifically taught." Spencer also found the draftsmen recognized perspective drawings faster. This study turns the cross-cultural literature on its head. If Spencer is correct, advanced technological conventions are less well understood by their users than are standard drawings based on everyday optics.

Cross-Species Research on Pictures

Hochberg and Brooks (1962) showed that an untutored child can identify pictures at the age of two years. An enterprising follow-up study showed that monkeys are as sensitive to some aspects of pictures as humans. Zimmerman and Hochberg (1963) trained a monkey to respond in one way to two triangles and to respond in a different way to a truncated solid pyramid. Then the monkeys were confronted with line drawings (see Fig. 14). The lines in different drawings correspond to the edges of the different forms on which the monkeys had been trained. The monkeys performed as humans might, transferring their responses to the appropriate representations. Evidently it is not necessary to train monkeys in a convention for them to pick up information from line drawings.

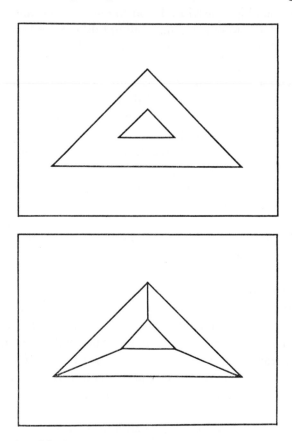

FIGURE 14. Monkeys responded to these drawings as they did to two triangles and a solid pyramid.

Monkeys have been known to put their heads close to pages on which watches were drawn, as though listening for ticking, and have been observed trying to pick up drawn objects. In one important case, a chimpanzee showed these responses without any training (Hayes and Hayes, 1953). And the chimp, named Viki, readily learned to imitate actions illustrated in pictures. The chimp was initially trained and tested on black and white motion pictures, then projected stills, then photographic prints, and finally simple line drawings. "She performed fairly well from the first session on, and transferred readily through the various stages from movies to line drawings. . . . she occasionally 'ran herself on the experiment' by plugging in the movie projector, or by getting pictures and spreading them out on the floor" (p. 471).

When tested further, Viki showed that she could accurately pick out pictures showing the same type of object as one held out by the experimenter, without the picture being an exact photograph or drawing of the experimenter's object. For example, the experimenter would hold out a toy car; then Viki would be asked to chose between a picture of another toy car or a picture of a flower. Viki would accurately pick out the picture of the car. Viki was not learning a limited set of symbols for a limited set of objects, for every test involved a new object and a new pair of pictures. On color pictures, negatives of pictures, and line drawings, Viki performed well, always with over 80 percent accuracy.

Even the lowly pigeon may have accurate picture perception. Herrnstein and Loveland (1964) trained pigeons to peck when they saw a photograph containing human beings and to refrain from pecking when confronted with a photograph not containing human beings. Each day of training, the slides were changed, or if some slides were being shown for a second time, the order was changed. "Many slides [even] contained human beings partly obscured by intervening objects—trees, automobiles, window frames, and so on. The people were distributed throughout the pictures—in the center, or to one side or the other, near the top or to the bottom, close up or distant. Some slides contained a single person, others contained groups of various sizes. The people themselves varied in appearance—they were clothed, seminude, or nude; adults or children; sitting, standing or lying; black, white, or yellow" (p. 550). Within ten training sessions the pigeons had begun to distinguish the two kinds of slides, and performance improved steadily and remained accurate when all the slides were made black and white as a test.

Some studies have used pictorial techniques in the investigation of problems not directly relevant to pictures. For example, Miller, Caul, and Mirsky (1967) and Miller (1967) allowed Rhesus monkeys to observe each other by television pictures. It was found that, without training, monkeys could react appropriately to facial expressions of monkeys depicted on television monitors. (In this case, the pictures were moving, of course, which may be a big help.)

Davenport and Rogers (1971) trained two chimpanzees and an orangutan to match a visible object with an object available only to touch. Then the primates were required to match a photograph with an object available only to touch. The primates had no experience with photographs prior to the study. Yet correct choices ranged from 80 to 100 percent across forty different pictures, in various combinations and in different testing sessions. In various sessions with black and white photographs, the primates choices were 60-100 percent correct. Davenport and Rogers conclude emphatically that apes can take information from a photograph at first sight.

Drees reportedly did a study (Hess, 1970, p. 10) possibly demonstrating picture perception in an insect. Drees presented jumping spiders (Salticidae family) with a life-sized picture of their normal prey. The spiders jumped thirty to forty successive times at the picture, and when shown the picture later would jump again at the screen. The Drees study is mostly useful for raising doubts about interpreting research with animals. Picture perception would indeed cause the jumping spider to respond. But perhaps the cue for a jumping response is a mere snatch of color or a few spindly, leglike marks. If so, the jumping response does not require picture perception; it merely requires noticing an instance, not a representation, of the cue that releases jumping. When a student sees a line drawing of a circle, he sees an instance of a circle. When he sees a line drawing of a cube, he sees a cube depicted—a picture of the cube. Thus, we have to be careful to distinguish "instances" from pictures.

The Drees study usefully shows that it is necessary to be cautious before we interpret studies of picture perception with animals. The subjects may be responding to small parts of the picture and genuine instances of things, not to the whole picture or an object that is depicted. This caution must be applied most stringently when reflexive or instinctual behaviors are considered, for such behaviors are often tied to quite minor features of objects. European robins will attack any small red fluffy object. Stickleback fish will threaten almost any red object when a mating mood is on them. It is not necessary to suppose the robins and sticklebacks genuinely perceive a whole complete member of their species, even though they attack the red objects. To give an analogy, it is more likely they are upset by red things in the automatic way that the screech of chalk on a blackboard can send shivers along one's spine.

When a chimp puts his ear down to a picture of a watch, with its circular form and numbers, but not to a picture of a ball or to a set of numbers alone, we are on reasonable ground attributing this to picture perception. When he identifies members of the class exemplified in a picture, this is better evidence. When his identification is made tactually, though the picture was available to sight, the argument is stronger. When pigeons behave differently to almost any slide containing humans than to a slide not containing humans, and the set of slides contains hundreds of instances, with humans often only partly visible, the argument is stronger yet. I think we may say that there is sound evidence showing picture perception exists in animals without training in conventions being necessary.

Summary

This attack on the theory that pictures are conventions has spanned two chapters, and a summary is in order.

It seems that pictures can provide accurate information, to the point of deception, which suggests some pictures are not based on arbitrary conventions. It seems, too, that children can identify some pictures without training in a convention, though it may be some months or years before pictorial skills develop spontaneously. On the basis of the evidence on *trompe l'oeil,* on the accuracy of pictorial judgments, and on spontaneous recognition in children, we may be suspicious of the popular view that nonpictorial people are baffled by photographs and other pictures. Both anecdote and systematic investigations show that people from a wide variety of cultures identify line drawings and photographs of objects similarly and even see comparable ambiguities in pictures. Different cultures favor different interpretations of ambiguous drawings or comment in different ways on the significance of frozen postures.

The hypothesis that pictures require training in a convention seems even less likely when it becomes evident that lowly pigeons and monkeys, both, seem capable of picture perception, with no training, or the minimum of training that may be required to acquaint them with the testing procedure.

Chapter Six

Figure and Ground

We see things because light from the surfaces of things reaches our eye. Surfaces structure light by various means, notably by being colored differently in different areas. Where two differently colored areas are adjacent to one another, the division between the two is called a *contour*.

Contours are considered very important to perception. They are often supposed to be the basis of the perception of shape, via a visual mechanism that results in the appearance of a clear figure against a vaguer background or ground. Figure and ground can also result from drawn lines—by a line I mean two contours close together, enclosing a narrow strip of pigment—which makes figure and ground a more general phenomenon, and also makes lines useful tools for exploring figure and ground.

The originator of the concepts of figure and ground was Edgar Rubin, a Dane. Despite the acclaim accorded his work, today his research is widely misunderstood. I will try to establish what he actually said, and contrast his work with today's mistaken interpretations. Then I will try to show that though Rubin may have described figure and ground appropriately, he failed to interpret them correctly. I will also try to show that Rubin misunderstood his own research because he failed to understand picture perception.

Rubin and His Inheritors

Rubin's research was first presented at length in Danish, in a two-volume work, whose title *Synsoplevede Figurer* (1915) translated means *visually experienced figures* or *visual figures*. Since 1915 the research papers, theses, and texts that have made use of Rubin's work have probably grown into the thousands. Curiously, though, almost nowhere have Rubin's ideas been challenged. Rarely has any psychological concept met with more acclaim and less dispute.

In place of criticism, most authors make use of Rubin's work as a stepping-stone to other research problems, and Rubin's observations and conclusions go unquestioned. The direction taken by most of his inheritors is to suggest uses of, not problems with, Rubin's principles. It is suggested that a figure-ground concept is basic to perception, important to general psychology, fundamental to art, useful to architecture, and instructive to philosophy. For example, Wever (1927) wrote that "the greatest contribution to the theory of visual form perception is the study by Edgar Rubin, in which the fundamental type of form experience was found to consist of a figure standing upon a ground" (p. 194). In a similar vein, Weintraub and Walker (1966) asserted that "probably the most basic organization imposed on the world by objects is that which leads to perception of objects as seeming to stand out against a background" (p. 9). Vernon (1939) in different words gave the same degree of emphasis: "Perception consists essentially in the emergence of the figure from the ground" (p. 91).

As the acclaim has grown, so too have the demonstrations of what are supposed to be the principles of figure and ground. Figure 15, which is adapted from Hochberg (1964, p. 59), is a version of a very interesting demonstration devised by Metzger

(1936). The demonstration figure is said to contain a word, but a word that goes undetected because of figure-ground principles. The typical observer says he sees a set of irregular blocks and does not see any letters, let alone a complete word. The observer puzzles over the display for a long time before finding the hidden word. If he was not told there was a word to find he might never notice it.

Told the identity of the hidden word the observer usually finds it quickly. It is the word FIGURE, whose letters appear "between the blocks," as it were. The observer usually comments that for some reason he did not think the spaces between blocks were relevant. He says he did not notice the shapes of the spaces between the blocks. Somehow, the shapes of the spaces were not evident in his experience, only the shapes of the meaningless blocks. One might say *the shape of the area on one side of the lines in the figure was not perceived.*

Consider another case where the shape on one side of a line is not perceived. In Fig. 16 there is a line that can be seen as having a shape like a profile. Observers can be asked to look at the figure and describe the profile they see. Some observers will notice a face with a long nose and a small, tightly closed mouth. Others will deny seeing any long-nosed face and will see a small nose and a gaping, distraught-looking mouth.

Both a long-nosed profile and a snub-nosed profile are present in Fig. 16, one facing to the left, the other to the right. But observers do not see both at once. At first, only one is seen, and the other is simply not evident. Then the other profile comes to view, and the first one becomes less evident. The two faces may fluctuate, one and then the other alternating. At the same time, quite remarkable changes occur in the appearance of the areas on either side of the line. First one area appears closer to the observer, and then the other area is closer. All the while, the steadfast lines on paper are constant and unchanging. The fluctuations are the observer's, not the display's.

One more example, this one adapted from Rubin, is shown in Fig. 17. Observers can be asked to see a black Maltese cross, and they will then see a black cross standing out against a more-distant white background. Or they can be asked to see a white Maltese cross, and then the black area will seem to be a more-distant background. The black and white crosses can alternate, and the shape of a Maltese cross at first seems to be evident in the black areas, and then the white areas, then in the black areas again, and so on.

The shapes of letters could be missed when blocks were seen in Fig. 15. The shape of a face could be absent when an observer looks at Fig. 16. An area could be seen with the shape of a cross at one moment and be mere background the next in Fig. 17. The shape of an area on one side of a line or contour is sometimes noticed, and sometimes seems like background. The area appears to be different at different times. These differences in the appearance of the same area at different times we might think were due to differences in attention. But Rubin found that attention was not the explanation.

We might think that the direction of our attention would affect whether we see the letters in Fig. 15, or the appearances of the crosses in Fig. 17, but this is not so. Rubin pointed out we can look directly at the spaces between the blocks in Fig. 15 and still not observe the letters. And we can look at a "background" area in Fig. 17, and the other area can still be "the cross." Shape can be retained by an area we are not holding in the center of our attention. Shape can be absent in areas that we make the center of our attention. So it is not our attention that makes shape appear and disappear from our experiences. Attention tells us where to look, as it were, but it does not always tell us what we see when we look there.

Furthermore, differences in distance—like an area in Fig. 16 becoming background and looking more distant—are not normally related in any way to attention. If we were to come down some rickety stairs very carefully, when we reached the stable ground again and stopped paying attention to our feet, they would not suddenly seem to grow more distant. Differences in the distance of parts of Fig. 16 cannot be explained by attention.

What Rubin seemed to have shown was that contours and lines could be seen as "having shape on only one side" and that this one-sided shaping effect was not simply due to attention. The area with shape he called "figure" and the adjoining area he called "ground." "To characterize the fundamental difference between the two," Rubin said, "it is useful to consider the contour, which is defined as the common boundary of . . . two fields. One can then state as a fundamental principle: When two fields have a common

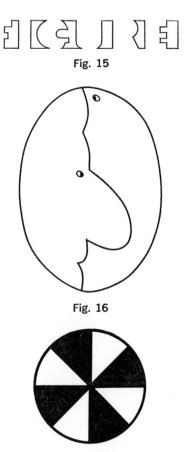

Fig. 15

Fig. 16

Fig. 17

FIGURE 15. Is there a word hidden here? The first impression is usually of a set of irregular blocks, shaped by the lines of the figure, and the spaces between the blocks look like general background. After a time, observers report seeing the word "figure" in the display. When the lines shape the blocks and not the spaces in between, they are said to have "one-sided" shaping effects.

FIGURE 16. A face with a long nose and a small, tightly closed mouth? Or with a small nose and a gaping, open mouth? The face-like area often seems more solid than the adjacent areas of the display. (Notice that the texture of the paper the figure is printed on is not seen as the texture of the face.)

FIGURE 17. A black cross against a white background can vary to look like a white cross against a black background. The crosses always seem nearer than the backgrounds, and both the crosses and their backgrounds often seem to be located at indefinite distances.

border, and one is seen as figure and the other as ground, the immediate perceptual experience is characterized by a shaping effect which emerges from the common border of the fields and which operates only on one field or operates more strongly on one than on the other" (1915, p. 35; 1958, p. 194).

At this point we have to begin to protect Rubin from his heirs. The claims Rubin made and the principle he described as fundamental were seen less clearly as time passed. As decades passed, psychology changed its moods and methods, and Rubin's phrases were refashioned to the needs of the moment. His ideas and his evidence became obscured behind inadvertently misleading re-interpretations.

At first, figure and ground seemed interesting and seemed to be useful for showing some relationships between contours, attention, and shape. Later, as the years went on, this important contribution to the study of perception became looked on, somewhat differently, as a study on an important part of perception. Later the emphasis shifted again, and figure and ground seemed more than important—the concept seemed basic to all of perception. Ultimately, writers stated flatly that figure and ground were necessary in perception.

To Rubin, figure and ground is interesting, a phenomenon that may have many implications. To Wever in 1927, Rubin had made a great contribution. By 1939, Vernon is saying that "perception consists essentially in the emergence of the figure from the ground" (p. 91). In 1949, Hebb first wrote, cautiously, "Simple figures do not always act as wholes innately. But it is undoubtedly true that they sometimes do so in one respect—in the figure-ground relationship" (p. 1). In continuing his discussion, the cautionary phrase "they sometimes do" seemed to vanish. He asserted, "The primitive unity [figure/ground] seems to be a direct product of the pattern of sensory excitation and the inherited characteristics of the nervous system" (p. 19). And, he continued, an area sensorily delimited "is seen as *one,* unified and distinct from its surroundings by any normal person, by the congenitally blind on the first occurrence of vision following operation for cataract (Senden, 1932), by the normal rat (Lashley, 1938), and apparently also at first vision by the rat that has been reared in darkness. The unity and distinctiveness of such figures from their background, then, is independent of experience, a "primitive" (pp. 19–20) . . . . There is a primitive or innate figure-ground mechanism (p. 21). The rat, as well as man, finds some figure-ground relations obvious and inescapable (p. 22)." Hebb makes a number of subtle and important points about attention and visual organization and figure-ground relations. But nothing that he says throws doubt on his strongly expressed view that Rubin's figure-ground phenomenon is the inescapable experience of human observers, young and old.

Woodworth's was a solitary voice in 1931, when he said that a figure was sure to occur if a contour was present. Hebb's writings became very influential, and probably as a result of his analysis of figure and ground now there is a great chorus avowing that figure and ground is necessary for any shape perception and an inescapable result of looking at a line or contour. Hochberg was expressing the will of the crowd (for example, Geldard, 1962; Pastore, 1971, p. 274; E. J. Gibson, 1969, p. 345) when he said: "Although any contour divides the stimulation at the eye into two regions, the shape of both regions cannot be simultaneously observed" (1964, p. 83).

The gradual drift from Rubin's description of figure and ground to flamboyant claims about the impossibility of seeing things any other way was not without good cause. First, the mood of researchers has changed from Rubin's gentle interest in describing a certain kind of experience people could have. Contemporary theorists want to describe causes for experience and have grown less concerned with contemplative attempts to analyze the details of individual experiences. Second, several demonstrations have seemed to show that past experience could not override a strong tendency to see "one-sided shaping effects."

Recall the FIGURE illustration (Fig. 15). Compare it to the WAX illustration and the FLY illustration of Figs. 18 and 19. It seems that despite our enormous familarity with the shapes of common letters, something interferes and prevents us seeing the meaningful configuration (the words) in favor of oddly shaped blocks. The figure-ground tendency entirely sweeps aside the influence of familiarity and meaningfulness. At any rate, that was the lesson drawn from these illustrations. The fact that it was impossible to see both faces at once in Fig. 16 has seemed further proof of the power of a figure-ground tendency.

Recall Fig. 17, a black cross on a white ground, or a white cross on a black ground, too. With figures such as these, Koffka (1935) claimed that it is difficult to see them as eight adjacent slices. The figure-ground tendency is too powerful for anything other than one-sided shaping effects to occur.

Two experiences made me suspicious of this interpretation of figure and ground laws. I showed the Maltese cross figure to a friend, who told me it looked like a beach ball. To her, the black and white wedges seemed like the eight adjacent panels on a ball.

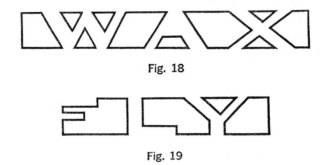

Fig. 18

Fig. 19

FIGURE 18.   The word wax is hidden here.

FIGURE 19.   The word fly is hidden here.

There seems to be no difficulty in seeing the figure this way. Once the hint is given, subjects say the figure looks like a beach ball as readily as it can look like Maltese crosses.

I also showed a line figure—a circle—to a few children ages five to nine. A figure and ground tendency, Rubin once suggested, might be present, weakly, in young children. Over the years this idea became transformed, until now whole schools of psychologists are said to believe that "the first phenomena experienced by the infant are qualities, or figures, upon a ground" (Bond, 1972, p. 226). I told the children to call the inner area of the circle "the island" and the outer area "the sea." I asked whether the island seemed to go under the sea, or the sea under the island, at the border or line. Sometimes, I called the inner area a lake and the outer area land, and asked the same questions. Adults who try this question report that the area which is figure seems closer, and the background extends behind the figure. The circular line only shapes the figure.

The children seemed to find my question meaningless. They would look at the drawing, but not answer. Any time they answered, it was after looking off to the side, seeming to think about the question, as though looking at the display was no help. Never did I find a child who could glance at the drawing and quickly reply. Figure and ground seemed not to be powerful in their experience.

I came to wonder whether there was not something wrong with analyses of the FIGURE, FLY, and WAX illustrations and the two-faced figure. The lesson to be drawn from the Maltese beach ball was that an appropriate hint would facilitate seeing borders as having shape on both sides. Would that work with the two-faced figure? Perhaps Fig. 20 provides the answer. Fig. 20 can be seen as a clam (or a thin-lipped hamburger!), with the dividing line shaping both top and bottom shells of the clam. Evidently, hints create and destroy the context for two-sided effects to occur. The "faces" hint prevented two-sided effects, perhaps, because seeing two faces fitting together is implausible, too difficult to imagine. The "clam" hint creates the correct context.

Hints about the letters reversed the FIGURE, WAX, and FLY figures, also. But why was it so difficult to see the letters in the first place? Is it true that figure-ground overwhelms the power of familiarity and meaningfulness? Perhaps the demonstration has been misanalyzed. Perhaps the rule that "contours are normally seen as one sided" has been incorrectly drawn from these figures. The fact is that *the letters are not present in these illustrations.* The letters are incomplete. Tops and bottoms are missing, and the shapes of the letters are oversimplified at times, so that important features are missing. And the terminations that are usually present at the tops and bottoms of letters are also absent. Fig. 21 restores some of these, and the result is blatantly obvious letters. These illustrations have been interpreted in ways that confuse the normal functions of contours in perception with the results of making shapes incomplete.

The modern version of Rubin's figure-ground principles was

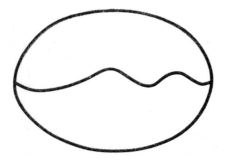

Fig. 20

Fig. 21

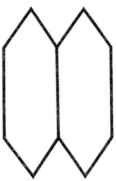

Fig. 22

FIGURE 20. When this figure is seen as a clam, the central line shows the shape of the upper and lower shells, meeting at the crack between the shells. Both the upper and lower shells look as solid as the crosses and faces seen in earlier illustrations.

FIGURE 21. Restoring missing parts to the Figure, Wax, and Fly illustrations makes the letters distinct. The absence of critical parts of the letters—such as interior detail, tops and bottoms of letters, and terminations—not a basic tendency to see lines as one sided, hid these words in earlier illustrations.

FIGURE 22. Two adjoining crystals or two overlapping crystals?

that figure-ground is inevitable if a line or contour is present. The popular demonstrations of figure-ground inevitability are readily reversed by hints and by supplying missing parts to misanalyzed illustrations. Was there any basis for the misguided modern version of Rubin's principles in his original research? Unfortunately not. With Elizabeth Kennedy I have examined Rubin's work in the original Danish version, and reviewed many of his research papers, published and unpublished, in the Danish Archives. Nowhere does he seem to find or suggest that contours necessarily give rise to figure and ground. Positive support for the idea is conspicuously absent. Instead, there are frequent reports that the occasional subject would see his displays with figure on both sides of a contour.

There is no difficulty in creating figures where lines shape both adjoining areas. Consider Fig. 22. Even without any hints, subjects see this as containing a line shaping two adjoining regions. The figure seems like two six-sided crystals. Each crystal is bounded or shaped by the middle line.

Consider a very clear case, in which lines give impressions of many different kinds of boundaries. Some of the impressions are figure-ground in type, some have shape on both sides of the line, and there are other shaping functions, too. Figure 23 is a line drawing that looks like a fence, with wires and cracks. Notice that lines that separate boards in the fence are seen as having figure on both sides; the lines mark the edges of surfaces of both adjoining boards. This is an important case: Rubin and others have suggested that if the ground does have shape, and if shape is perceived on both sides of a border, the ground would be shaped by borders it does not have in common with the figure. In fact, in the above example adjoining boards in the fence are shaped by borders they share in common. Other lines shape the top of the posts, giving the figure-ground appearance of a nearby board and a distant background. Others shape the interior of boards, showing where the front meets the slanting top.

The lines that seem like wires are cases where neither region adjoining the wire is figure, only the line itself. (Kaplan, 1969, with animated movies of moving textures, often found boundaries between regions of texture seemed to "stand out" from either adjoining region, looking appreciably closer to the observers than either

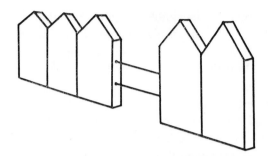

FIGURE 23. A fence, with wires, cracks, corners, and edges all shown by lines. Some of the lines give figure-ground impressions, others give shape to both adjoining areas, and some shape to neither of the adjoining areas. Depth and slant can be seen; at the same time it is clear that all the lines are in the same plane. Notice too, how the texture of the paper is not relevant to the texture of the figure or the ground.

of the adjoining regions. That is, the boundary was a figure on its own, quite apart from the adjoining regions, just like the wires in Fig. 23. Rubin found ways to make a contour alone be figure; that is, he found ways to make a contour seem to stand out, elevated from the adjoining colored regions.)

To round out the discussion at this point, I will summarize the main points before delving more deeply into Rubin's ideas. Figure and ground, as described by Rubin, is one of the possible shaping effects of lines or contours. In contrast to his inheritors' views, Rubin did not think and prove that figure and ground were necessary results of the presence of a visible contour or line. Figure-ground demonstrations are strongly affected by hints, and demonstrations of the power of a figure-ground tendency were actually showing the influence of removing and altering parts of familiar shapes.

Rubin's Characterization of Figure and Ground

Rubin noticed that when two areas of different color met at a contour or an area is divided in two by a line, an observer of the two areas might see them as differing in more ways than color and location. I will describe the differences he noticed, some factors he found influenced figure and ground, and some factors he found seemed strangely irrelevant. Rubin offers a careful description of figure-ground differences and influences, which I will try to explain here.

Much of Rubin's work was descriptive. He was a phenomenologist; that is, he tried to establish the characteristics of a certain kind of visual experience. It is these characteristics and their significance that have least been questioned by later authors. I will suggest, following some leads by Gibson (1951), that their customary interpretation as basic in normal perception is in need of a complete revision.

The fundamental difference between figure and ground Rubin characterized as one area having shape belonging to the common contour and the other area having no shape from the common contour. The area shaped by the common contour he called figure; the other area he called ground. The contour limited the figure, and not the ground. The ground even seems to extend behind the figure (1915, pp. 36–37).

The figure was said to have the character of "a thing." A thing he considered to be a material with shape. The ground seemed more like a "substance." He compared "things" and "substances" to an aspect of language as follows. We can take a material-word, add it to a shape-word, and get a thing-word! *Water* plus *drop* becomes *waterdrop; gold* plus *bar* becomes *gold-bar* (p. 44)—these were two examples he gave. To Rubin, then, a thing is a unified whole, a bounded lasting shape (p. 45) made of some substance—a substance with definite shape.

The ground looks like a substance, not a thing, in the way that expanses of sand or flour seem like substances. But the substance of the ground is *not* the same as the substance of the paper or screen used for making the display (p. 44). The texture of the surface of the display can be quite distinct from the apparent substance of the ground. Why the material of the display should be irrelevant is a question I will try to answer later.

By having shape, the figure was more ornate and distinct than the ground; its features were more likely to be noticed (leading Rubin's predecessors to conclude erroneously that paying attention created the impression of shape in the figure). The figure was prominent both in the sense of being more likely to be examined by his subjects, and also it "stood out." Its localization was somewhat indefinite; observers found they did not have a clear impression of its distance. All they could say was that it stood out in front of the ground. Its indefinite localization is a puzzle. Why is there anything indefinite at all about the distance of a contour on a piece of paper? I will also tackle this question later.

When an area is seen as figure and later as ground, its color seems to change, too. As a figure, Rubin found the color would appear more compact, and look as though it were on a surface. Katz (1935) previously had noticed this appearance and he called it surface color. As a ground, a color would seem filmy or airy like the sky, less compact. In Katz's terms, these are film or volume colors.

Rubin said that subjects were more likely to "put something into" the figure than "into" the ground (p. 69). One striking example may help make part of his meaning clear. One subject "put something into" adjoining areas of a display. The display was "seen as" a green mushroom on which a black worm was crawling. Rubin said that the subject would "put into" a display things with similar shapes to the figure. Hence the ground, having no perceived shape, would not have "things put into it" (pp. 71, 79, and Chap. 9). The subject may also recall some event that happened to occur when he first saw one of Rubin's displays. Recalling the extraneous event when the display is shown again Rubin describes as "putting it into the experience of the display." Subjects can put form and motion or events into their experience of the display.

Besides describing the characteristics of figure and ground, Rubin investigated the role played by figure and ground in essential skills such as recognition and also investigated some factors influencing which areas would more likely be seen as figure. I will not reinterpret some of these investigations, but will note them in passing.

If an area of a display was seen as figure on the first presentation of the display, that area would be figure again on the second presentation, Rubin found. With some displays, different subjects could be instructed to see different areas of the displays as figure on the first showing of the display. On a second showing, the same area would be figure.

With the same kinds of displays, Rubin could instruct subjects to see different areas as figure at different times. He found that if subjects saw a different figure the second time a display was shown (that is, if figure and ground were reversed), the display was not recognizable. Zusne (1970, p. 121) notes that debate over this finding has concluded in favor of Rubin.

Among the factors determining which area would be seen as figure were these six: (1) The enclosing area was more likely to be figure. (2) The instructions or attitudes given to the subject were important. (3) The lower area would more likely be figure. (4) Vertical and horizontal figures were preferred over diagonal figures. where vertical and horizontal were taken in relation to a framework like the sides of the page or screen used for the display. (5) If one area contained distinctive marks of a well-known thing or had the shape of a familiar object, it was likely to be figure. (6) Some colors were preferred over others.

One can attend to the ground and describe its characteristics. The ground is therefore not merely an unattended part. The differences between figure and ground are qualitative, not merely differences in vagueness or clarity. The change between figure and ground, with a given area, is usually surprising to subjects and unlike the effect of seeing something in the periphery and turning to examine it. So Rubin concluded the differences between figure and ground cannot be explained by differences in the direction of attention.

Rubin leaves us a list of differences between figure and ground, some evidence on the role of figure and ground in recognition and the observation that differences in the direction of attention do not explain figure and ground.

Earlier we noted the way hints influence the perception of figure and ground, and Rubin too noticed how instructions can change figure and ground and vice versa. He also noticed that some characteristics of a display such as its texture, may have no role in figure and ground. It may be that Rubin played down the role of attention a little too much. It may be that there is more to attending than a change in the direction of attention. It may be that hints and instructions can control markedly different ways of looking.

Gibson's Pictorial Perception and Figure-Ground

In the early 1950's, J. J. Gibson distinguished between different ways of looking. Consider some of his points that may have a bearing on figure and ground. In a 1951 paper entitled "What is a form?" Gibson argued that often the marks we make on surfaces can be taken as depictions of the edges of surfaces. The perception afforded by these marks is a special kind. "The paper surface is scarcely seen and a different surface seems to emerge within the outline. The paper surface appears to become 'background.' . . . Most observers perceive an object and do not see tracings on a surface at all" (pp. 405–406).

Gibson is perhaps not the phenomenologist Rubin was. The paper surface is, of course, clearly visible—to say it is not seen is too strong. The notion of a surface emerging within the outline is perhaps misleading; it sounds like slow condensation, quite unlike the immediate impressions of shape given by many displays. The paper surface may well look like a foreground or a framework instead of background. I doubt if observers fail to see that what they look at is tracings on a surface.

Happily, the key to Gibson's insight lies not in these misleading observations but in a fact that Gibson noticed and Rubin overlooked. Gibson noticed that with these kinds of displays, "when you press the question, [subjects] tell you that they do not literally see a physical object, but a picture of it" (p. 406).

Rubin never pressed Gibson's question onto his subjects. In fact, Rubin gave his subjects very curious instructions: He told them to report what they saw, not what they knew. Let us closely consider the relationship between the perceiver and the displays. Rubin's instructions probably biased his subjects toward leaving out of their reports many things that were obviously true about the displays. The instructions indicate that Rubin, too, was biased, that he probably took far more interest in reports about the displays that were obviously not true, things that because they were not true he could ascribe to perception and not to cognition. In other words, Rubin asked about "experiences" but was never blunt enough to say "list the physical characteristics of my displays that you can see to be true," a request that might have allowed him to distinguish between perception of the display and perception of the display as a depiction.

Rubin never pushed his subjects for accurate descriptions of the displays. Perhaps when subjects said things like "The figure seems to be on top of the ground," they could actually have told Rubin that it was obvious, too, all the while that the figure area was actually no nearer than the ground area, that all of the color patches were on the same plane. Consider the illustrations on the preceding pages; they were accompanied by words like "beach ball," "boards," "wires," and "cracks" (and these were appropriate captions). But if anyone had been asked to list the physical characteristics of the display, there is no doubt what he would have said. He would have mentioned black and white patches, lines and contours, and that is all. Someone might say the boards in the fence are thick, or the beach ball round, or the figure in front of the ground. But, if pressed, he would have said, too, that he was seeing black and white areas, flat, all in the same plane.

Rubin noticed similarities between perception of real physical surfaces with edges and perception of line or contour figures. Gibson noticed there were differences as well (though, as I pointed out, some of the differences he describes are questionable). Rubin was not blind to the fact that subjects could say that a display could look like something other than what it was or reminded subjects of extraneous events or extraneous scenes like a worm crawling on a mushroom. In fact, Rubin promised a third section to his thesis (which was hurried because of the duties of war) on the fact that sometimes subjects "put things into" a display, as he phrased it. This third section was written, in rough draft, and perhaps incompletely. We may never know his final position, because as a result of yet another war the notes and drafts were lost, and not all his papers have been recovered. (Elizabeth Kennedy was given much-appreciated help by Danish archivists, psychologists, and Rubin's family in searching through Rubin's papers, but without recovering that vital third section.)

In Rubin's phrase, "putting into a display," one can see his cautious approach to the possibility of the displays being depictions. But his approach always remains superficial in the 1915 work. Notice that he claimed that an area containing features of a well-known object would be likely to be figure. And he went on to claim that subjects can "put into figures" things like well-known objects or movements. But he never discusses the bases for "putting something into a figure." He does not offer criteria for distinguishing what is "put into" a figure from what is seen there. Nor does he distinguish what is "put in" because the display is a picture from what is "put in" on entirely fortuitous grounds. The subject may remember some chance event—a cough, a door slamming—that occurred when a display was shown. Recalling the chance event when the display occurs again is called, by Rubin, "putting it into the experience of the display."

On the one hand, Rubin fails to distinguish pictorial properties of the display from chance associations with the display. On the other hand, his descriptions of the experiences resulting from his displays are distinguished from "things put into the display" on purely intuitive, completely unstated grounds. Gibson's request that the subjects separate what is truly there from what they see the display is depicting (and from what the display happens to remind them of) could be the beginning of an effort to make Rubin's intuitive distinctions explicit. The cost of the effort will be that figure and ground will be considered part of a very complex kind of perception (no longer the simple basis of perception). Consider that displays unmistakably made solely of lines can be seen as beach balls, boards in a fence, cracks, or wires. The display is seen as made of lines and also, at the same time, as objects that the observer can see are not present. The observer can tell that the difference in depth between figure and ground is apparent, not real. Is figure and ground a pictorial phenomenon? If so, the differences between figure and ground should be more than a list of unrelated items. They should follow from the nature of depiction.

Figure-Ground as Pictorial Perception

So, can most of the figure-ground experience be explained as perception of the displays as pictures?

Perhaps a contour or line on a display can be seen as depicting the edge of a surface—the silhouette of an irregular object, isolated, in front of some background. The ground is then the area on one side of the line or the contour representing the background which extends behind the near surface. The apparent depth difference is present simply because the contour or line represents the edge of a near surface, against a background. Since the background could be either another extended surface or empty air without visible structure (like the sky), the area seen as ground could represent something or nothing, as the subject chooses or is instructed or is informed about by parts of the display, and will be reported by the subject accordingly.

When both areas are figure, the contour or line represents not an isolated object against a background but two adjacent surfaces—as in a case where a subject saw the display as being "like interlocking fingers" (Rubin, p. 12). Then, too, the subject need not see a display as representing anything at all, but as simply adjacent areas of differing color (some of Rubin's subjects reported this with some displays). Naturally, then, the figures would have the character of things. For it is precisely bounded surfaces—which Rubin *defines* as things—that are reported as being experienced. And the color of the figure would, in Katz's terms, be reported as surface color, for it is precisely surfaces that are represented.

Rubin noticed that the characteristics of the ground need not depend on the materials used in the display. The consistency of his linen projection screen, or the paper on which displays are printed, is irrelevant. The consistency and texture is evident to subjects but plays no role in the figure-ground experience. Rubin does not explain the null role of the surface texture of the display. But that null role is significant if the figure-ground experience is inherently pictorial. If the display is taken to be a picture, it is usually taken to have only some significant pictorial features—its flatness, for example, or its color (like the black of a blackboard) are irrelevant. Texture—as in the smoothness of a blackboard, the grain of a piece of paper, and the weave of a linen projection screen—is also irrelevant. Only marks that seem to be due to artifice, such as lines and contours of painted areas, are taken to be relevant to depiction. In the absence of such artificial marks the ground would not be reported as having any particular texture. In the presence of such artificial marks *the ground does have texture* (Koffka, 1935, p. 194), as a pictorial theory would predict.

Rubin also noticed that the figure and the ground seemed "indefinitely" located. Their distance from the observer was unspecific, though the ground seemed further than the figure. Rubin did not explain these experiences of location. But if the contour or line represents an edge of a surface against a background, the nearness of the figure is understandable. And the indefiniteness of the location of both figure and ground can be understood, too. The indefiniteness is puzzling only if we try to think of figure and ground as typical of some basic process in normal perception. Because subjects can, of course, tell exactly how far the surface of the display is, with its lines and contours. The distance is not further than the screen or book or page the subject is being shown. That distance is not at all imprecise to subjects. Then why should the figure and ground emerging from the lines and contours in the display be indefinitely located? How can it be that the lines and contours are clearly located and that the figure and ground are not? The answer could be that figure and ground are inherently pictorial, and the display as a picture does not provide information about the location of the figure and ground. The lines or contours are precisely located, but what they depict is not, without additional information.

Many of Rubin's proposals for factors influencing which area would be seen as figure make sense if the displays are considered as pictures. If one is to take the lines and contours as depicting the edges of surfaces, then the particular area adjacent to an irregular line or contour that will represent a surface is equivocal in the absence of further information. So it makes sense to find that subjects can adopt a set to perceive either one side or another as representing a surface. That the lower area is typically taken as representing a surface might follow from the fact that most surfaces in the world are on the terrain in the world, not up in the sky. That the area containing distinctive marks of a known object is seen as figure follows directly from a pictorial hypothesis about figure and ground. If one area has the outline shape of a well-known object and the other does not, it follows, too, that the well-known object would more likely be seen.

The factors of color or reflectance (Botha, 1963) and enclosure or size (Oyama, 1960), or the preference for vertical figures rather than diagonal figures, can perhaps be less readily subsumed under a pictorial hypothesis, but these very factors are not more than "tendencies"—they are not particularly powerful in their effect, and they are readily reversed by hints. Nor do they explain the characteristics of the figure-ground experience, and it is these characteristics and their significance that are at issue.

Shape on one side of a border at one time, shape on both sides of a border at other times, unreal (to the subject) differences in depth, the irrelevance of the consistency of a display, the mixture of precise location of contours or lines and indefiniteness of the location of figure and ground—these and other reports from Rubin's subjects all make sense only if subjects can see simple irregular lines and contours as depictions of the edges of surfaces. Investigators have generally thought that simple line and contour displays should be used to investigate the basic laws of perception. It may be that typically subjects see these displays as pictures as well as simple forms, as Gibson (1951) suggested. The simplicity of the forms allowed ambiguity: it was deceptive and allowed subjects to take a pictorial attitude.

One can still learn a great deal from Rubin's subjects. They did not behave erratically. There are common threads to their reports. What they tell us, though, is not about a mysterious figure-ground tendency that is necessary to all forms of perception. They tell us about a special way of looking, in which a line or contour depicts the edge of a surface. Rubin's subjects provide the first systematic evidence ever gathered on the puzzle of line and contour representation. What remains to be done is to explore the possibilities of line and contour representation yet further. The next step is to ask what lines or contours can represent.

This chapter was on the legacy left by a very impressive set of studies by Edgar Rubin. Rubin was very angry with the ways in which his work was abused by his readers (MacLeod, 1968). This chapter tried to show how the times have indeed mistreated his work and tried to clarify his original intentions. But his work has to be reunderstood, for it is actually a beginning study on picture perception. The next chapter will go beyond Rubin's research and try to answer the question his work seems to point to—namely, what can a line depict?

Chapter Seven

The Scope of Outline Pictures

*P*eople who live a few miles apart, in neighboring countries (such as France and Germany), often do not understand each other, for though they use the same elements of speech—that is, the same sounds—the combinations of sounds often mean nothing to the listener. Of course, the elements alone—isolated sounds—mean nothing to either speaker or listener. The same is true with written words. As separate elements, W, O, R, D are only nondescript letters, and together they mean *word* only to someone familiar with English. It is clear that to be familiar with a language one must acquire a huge vocabulary, for each word may mean something different; to know the elements of a new word, or words like it, will not help one to understand the word.

But in any country and in any age since the cave artists, once a man has learned about sketching he can, if he wants, represent things to his neighbors (Chapter 5), his children (Chapter 4), and even some of his pets (Chapter 5). Why is it that mere lines can be so versatile? What are some rules that could explain their usefulness to people from different backgrounds?

Elements of the Visible Environment

Logically, if lines can depict the basic elements that create a visible environment, then lines could have the power to depict anything that was visible. Perhaps every visible object and every scene is made of the combinations and arrangements of a few essential elements. The same essential elements and the same kinds of combinations may occur throughout the world. Can lines depict such elements? If so, the usefulness of line drawings across cultures would be understandable. Such elements would be properties of the environment that influence the light coming to the eye. They would be the elements about which light might provide information. Varying the order or layout of the elements would result in different objects, different landscapes, the entire visible world. And if line depiction is tied to some of the fundamental features of the visible environment, that would help explain why vision research such as Rubin's inevitably became caught up in problems of depiction.

In one conception, the elements of vision are patches of color, stimulated by light of different wavelengths. This is a traditional and standard conception of vision, but it is not useful for analyzing depiction, because depiction, and outline depiction especially, usually violates the colors of the depicted objects. A black-and-white sketch might depict a rainbow among the clouds, over a grassy field. Nowhere in the sketch would the colors of the rainbow be portrayed. To match the colors of the depicted object is a rare achievement in illustrations. It is necessary to find some other conception than color to describe elements of vision.

Another conception of vision could treat each object (or pattern) as an element. In this view, each object is an independent unit, and an arrangement of objects forms a scene—just as a still life is a scene made up of domestic objects, each independent of its neighbors, as well as all being together in one place. Verbal discourse involves fairly independent units—the various words we use. But depictions of two different objects are more alike than are two different words. We can draw a picture of an unfamiliar object for a friend, and he will recognize the object if it eventually appears. When we simply tell our friend the name for the object, he cannot usually recognize the object when it appears. A picture of an unfamiliar object can tell our friend how many legs the object has, where its arms and neck are, and so on. Presumably, the picture tells our friend about familiar visual elements in a new arrangement. If so, pictures represent parts of objects, not just the whole object.

So, are the basic elements of pictures the parts of objects? Think of pictures of animals; the parts include arms, hooves, necks, ears, and the like. Indeed, these parts make up the animals, as elements of the whole animal. But different kinds of objects are made of different parts: animals are made of hooves, limbs, torsos, and so on; suitcases are made of flaps, handles, locks, and the like; wine glasses are made of brims, stems, etcetera. There is an infinite variety of objects and an infinite variety of kinds of parts of objects. If the parts we have been mentioning were the basic elements in outline pictures, a large vocabulary of parts would be involved in understanding them. Perhaps there are more basic elements than the kinds of parts mentioned so far, some kinds of basic elements that are few in number.

If objects can be analyzed into a few basic elements, perceivers might use a small set of units—a small vocabulary—to understand any and all outline drawings.

Is there a small set of basic elements in the visible world? When the question is put another way, a small set of elements is suggested. Consider: Are there just a few elements that create the optic array at the eye? One such element is a contour, so popular in figure-ground research, where the pigmentation on a surface varies from one area of a surface to an adjoining area. Another is shadowing, where the illumination on a surface varies because an opaque object intervenes between part of the surface and the source of illumination on the surface. Another element is given by variation in the relationship between a smooth surface, the source of illumination, and the location of an observer—yielding highlights. Yet another is provided by variation in the inclination of a surface —some facets of a surface may face the direction of illumination more directly than others and so receive stronger illumination. And still another is created by varying surface texture.

These elements are the main sources of variation in an optic array and are the basic features of the visible environment. Varying the layout of surfaces creates hills and valleys and the shapes of objects. Variation in pigmentation creates the coloring of a landscape and its objects. Variation in the locations and opaqueness and smoothness of objects and the locations of sources of illumination creates shadows and highlights. Variations in the material of objects and the forces they are subject to creates different textures. Optic arrays contain the information for a visible environment, and, in the last analysis, it is variation in surfaces—their layout and composition and their relation to sources of illumination—that create optic arrays.

Variation in surfaces and their relation to sources of illumination provide the basic elements of the visible world. If lines in outline drawings can depict many or all of the sources of an optic array, then the versatility of outline sketches is understandable. The visibility of objects and landscapes, the entire visible world, rests in the main on a few sources of optic structure. If lines can depict each of the main sources of optic structure, then lines can depict almost any visible object or scene. And these would be not simply normal familiar objects, or familiar parts of objects, but anything that is visible except pure color and uniform surface—for arrangements of color patches on a surface may be outlined, but pure isolated colors or uniform surfaces cannot be.

Can each source of optic structure be depicted in outline drawings? Will an untrained subject be able to understand such outline depictions? Let us consider the elements of the visible world one by one.

Layout of Surfaces

Surfaces are either plane or curved. They can face toward or away from an observer, so a concept of a point of observation must be incorporated into any description of arrangements of visible surfaces.

One plane surface may join another plane surface at an

angle, with both surfaces being visible from a particular point of observation. The two surfaces form a two-sided plane angle, a dihedral angle as it is called in solid geometry. There are two types of dihedral angles. One type is *concave* to the point of observation, like the corner of a room (Fig. 24). The other type is *convex* to the point of observation, like the corner of a building (Fig. 25). An abrupt change in the inclination of visible surface occurs across a dihedral angle—a plane through the point of observation and the apex of the dihedral angle meets the two surfaces at sharply different inclinations.

One of two adjoining plane surfaces may not be visible from a point of observation because it is behind the other surface with respect to the point of observation (Fig. 26). The visible surface is the front surface, and it is said to *occlude* the other surface. A front surface occludes the back surface, and the visible terminations of the front surface are called *occluding edges*. The distance from the point of observation to sources of optic structure changes abruptly from one side of an occluding edge to the other. On one side of the occluding edge is the front surface and on the other side is background.

A different kind of occlusion occurs with curved surfaces. Instead of two plane surfaces meeting at a dihedral angle, one sur-

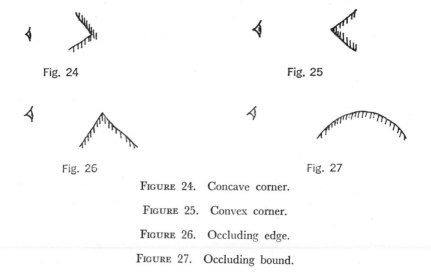

Fig. 24

Fig. 25

Fig. 26

Fig. 27

FIGURE 24. Concave corner.

FIGURE 25. Convex corner.

FIGURE 26. Occluding edge.

FIGURE 27. Occluding bound.

face gradually changes its inclination and joins the back side of the object smoothly, as in a sphere or the brow of a hill (Fig. 27). Again, the back side is occluded by the front surface. The surface layout is convex and rounded, not convex and angular. There is no edge, strictly speaking of a sphere; nevertheless, spheres can occlude. I will call the visible terminations of the front surface of rounded objects *occluding bounds*. A sphere has no edges, but it has occluding bounds. Any curved surface has occluding bounds when its tangent passes through the point of observation. There is an abrupt change in distance of surfaces from the point of observation on either side of the tangent from a point of observation to an occluding bound.

Beyond occluding surfaces lie backgrounds. A *background* lies behind an occluding edge or bound and does not make contact with the occluding surface. Occluding surfaces occlude not only their back surface but also parts of background surfaces. In some cases, the background is not another surface, as occurs when the sky is background. Whether the background is a surface or the sky, there is an abrupt change in distance from the point of observation on either side of a plane through an occluding edge or bound of any terrestrial object. On one side of the plane is the occluding surface, and on the other is the distant background.

Plane surfaces, curved surfaces, and dihedral angles are concepts of layout that are independent of any observer. When a point of observation is introduced, occluding edges, occluding bounds, and backgrounds result. Occluding edges and bounds and dihedral angles are visible features of surface layout. Arrangements of these features make up the visible terrain and objects standing on the terrain. Can an outline drawing depict some of these features? Which will be recognizable?

Cross-cultural research and research on children finds that the shapes of objects can be recognized in outline drawings. The shapes of objects are created by variation in the arrangement of plane and curved surfaces; shapes are arrangements of features of surface layout. So it seems that some of the features of surface layout are recognizable in outline drawings without training. And depictions of all the features of surface layout occur commonly in newspaper and textbook illustrations, in drawings from many cultures and times. Cave paintings are often in the form of outline drawings depicting the edges of objects and occluding bounds of objects. The most common use of outline depiction is depiction of features of surface layout—this is the usual vocabulary of the language of outline. It appears to be a language discovered by early man, universal in its understandability and inherent in the nature of man's visual perception, for it requires no training.

Fig. 28 is an attempt to incorporate into one picture outline depiction of all the features of surface layout. It should be instantly understandable to the normal Western reader. Words to describe it may be restricted to one culture, and the objects it depicts may be unfamiliar to some cultures, but the kind of features it shows should be identifiable in some line drawing or another by anyone reared in a world of solid objects that rest on a terrain that stretches to a horizon.

Figure 28 shows a seascape and a landscape with rounded hills and a house with a walled-in garden. Different segments of the lines in the figure depict the following six features: (1) An occluding bound with a background surface—the brow of a hill, with the surface of another hill behind. (2) An occluding bound with no background surface—the brow of a hill, with sky visible above the hill. (3) An occluding edge with no background surface—the apex of the roof of the house, with sky visible above the house. (4) An occluding edge with background surface—the termination of a wall, where the continuation of the surface of the wall is occluded by the near surface, with ground surface visible beyond the termination of the wall. (5) A dihedral angle forming a concave corner—two visible plane surfaces of wall meeting at an angle of less than 180 degrees, measured through the air enclosed by wall. (6) A dihedral angle forming a convex corner—two surfaces of the house meeting at an angle of more than 180 degrees, measured through the air around the surfaces.

As Fig. 28 shows, all the basic features of surface layout can be depicted by lines in outline drawings. A segment of line can depict an occluding edge or bound or a dihedral angle. What makes a segment of line depict at one time an occluding edge and at another time an occluding bound is the context in which it is viewed. The context can be other lines patterned around the line segment, as in Fig. 28, or the set of the observer, as pointed out in Chapter 6.

Besides the six features listed above, outline is capable of a seventh kind of depiction. Each of the basic features of surface layout is depicted by single lines in Fig. 28. However, sometimes a single line can depict more than one feature of surface layout. That is, representation of several features of surface layout can sometimes be achieved with the use of a single line. One example is contained in Fig. 28—namely, the crack between the door and the walls of the house. A crack results when two dihedral angles of two surfaces

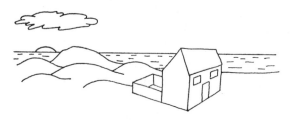

FIGURE 28. The meanings of a line. Seven kinds of referents are included in this figure.

abut or adjoin each other. Two abutting dihedral angles can be depicted by a single line.

Another example of a single line depicting more than one feature of surface layout was shown in Fig. 19, in Chapter 6. That figure depicted a fence with a gap between two of the boards bridged by strands of wire, each strand depicted by single wires. If the strands were depicted as very thick, as thick as ropes, two lines would be present, one line for each side of occluding bound of the thick strands. Depicted by single lines, the strands are shown as thin wires.

To depict a thick strand, two lines could be used. Similarly, to depict a wide crack, two lines could be used. Dihedral angles and occluding bounds are depicted by single lines only. Thus, there is a critical difference between strands and cracks and single features of surface layout. Strands and cracks are created by several features of surface layout, and in principle each feature can be depicted by single lines. Wires are cylinders, with parallel occluding bounds. Looked at closely, the cylinder would become evident. Cracks are

spaces, provided by parallel abutting dihedral angles. The interior
or background of the space could be made evident. But typically
the substance of the wire or the background of the space may be
indistinct. That is, optic structure from the material of a wire or
coming through a crack is often too fine to be registered. A general
rule suggested by line depiction of wires and cracks is as follows:
An arrangement of several features of surface layout can be depicted by a single line if the features are close together, parallel, and
the optic structure from the region between the outer margins is
not distinct. This general rule could cope with line representation
of cracks and wires, and it provides for grooves and scars and rail-
road tracks being depicted by single lines.

In sum, line segments in line configurations can depict the
basic features of surface layout—dihedral angles forming convex
and concave corners, and occluding edges and bounds, with or
without background surfaces, and single lines can also depict combinations of features that are close together and parallel, with indistinct internal detail. To rephrase, lines can depict discontinuities
of depth or slant, and single lines can depict combinations of these
discontinuities if the discontinuities are in parallel, close, and without distinct internal detail.

The Substance of Surfaces

The substance of surfaces is often capable of structuring the
light that comes to the eye. A surface can be smooth or planar and
yet entail substances that have different capacities to reflect light.
This difference in reflectance may be selective with regard to the
wavelength of light, in which case one part of the surface is said to
have a different color than other parts. Or the difference in reflectance may simply result in some areas being able to reflect more of
the incident light than others, in which case some areas are said to
be lighter than others. The differences in reflectance are said to be
due to differences in pigmentation. So a surface may have no layout discontinuities of distance or inclination and yet provide pigment discontinuities.

To show depiction of pigment discontinuities alone it is necessary to represent layout in which the only discontinuities are pro-

vided by change in pigmentation on a smooth surface. Pure cases of pigment change without surface-layout discontinuities occur in the coloration of animals. The wings of butterflies and the hides of animals are often sources of pure pigment discontinuities that do not correspond to surface-layout change. Can pigment discontinuities be recognized in outline depiction?

Figure 29 is an attempt to show pure pigment change. The object shown is an animal. If a subject recognizes Fig. 29 as an animal, a horse in particular, information about features of surface layout is being recognized. If a subject sees the figure as depicting a zebra, the interior lines of the figure are functioning as depictions of the pigment-change on the hide of the animal. If the subject were to see the figure as a horse with lines painted on its flanks, then the interior lines would not be acting as depictions of boundaries of areas of pigment. In informal fashion, dozens of adults and two children have been shown Fig. 29. All the adults, usually faculty and graduate students, have taken the figure to be a depiction of a zebra, and thus the interior lines depicted margins of areas of pigment. The two children, visitors to the Cornell psychology laboratory, had interesting reactions. One, a five-year-old girl, thought of the figure as a horse with lines on it. The other, her eight-year-old brother, not only saw the figure as depicting a zebra, but even spontaneously identified some areas as showing the shape of light or dark areas on the pictured zebra. The guiding principle he offered was that zebras are light on the underbelly, and from this knowledge he was able to figure out where the dark and light areas should be!

The adults and children were simply shown Fig. 29 and asked "What is this?" No explicit hints were given. Once they had responded, they were asked "What is this line for?" They were asked about lines for the back and legs of the zebra before being asked about an interior line. The figure was recognized as a zebra by the adults and by one child. It seems likely from this informal evidence that lines can depict pigment discontinuities without training in any convention.

Lines can depict changes in layout of surfaces and the layout of pigmentation on a surface. The context for a line is a critical factor in determining what a given line is depicting. The more un-

FIGURE 29. An outlined zebra containing lines depicting pigment boundaries.

familiar the context—the depicted configuration—the more difficult it may be to ensure that the observer sees only one definite feature of the environment as depicted by a given line. Presumably, the five-year-old girl who failed to see Fig. 29 as depicting a zebra was comparatively unfamiliar with zebras. Perhaps a depiction of a favorite pet cat with lines showing the shapes of the pet's markings would make the transfer from the solid, colored, textured, real world to the merely black-and-white line drawing easier. A drawing of a favorite costume, with its color patterns depicted only by lines, might be easily recognizable, too. Possibly the simplest thing would be to show examples of flags, like the American, British, and Canadian flags, in outline, omitting all color. Their distinctive patterns completely depend on pigment differences in otherwise uniform cloth.

Outline drawings restricting the observer to one unambiguous perception must usually both replay a highly specific optical structure and also capture the observer's understanding of environmental structure. Figure 29 seems to be specific enough for many subjects. Lines in the figure are identified as depicting pigment areas. The figure provides information about pigmentation without reproducing the full patchwork of a zebra. It seems that to identify a shape as an area of pigment one need not have all the coloring reproduced. Features of shape, without color, can be adequate. Informative features of the figure probably include, for example, the fact that none of the interior lines disturb the overall silhouette. The interior lines simply terminate at the exterior lines; they do not make exterior lines poke out, as gaunt ribs would. The exterior line is smoothly continuous. Thus, the interior lines do not indicate ribs and concavities, which would disturb the overall silhouette. The overall horse shape is probably critical, too. If the overall shape was not evident, the interior lines could easily be taken to be contours on a map. Many features of this zebra depiction are shared with other figures, but the zebra figure seems to include enough distinctive features to be specific to outline depiction of pigment areas. The lesson to be drawn is that outline depiction capitalizes on—and, if a depiction is to be unambiguous, is restricted to—visible features of the environment that have distinctive form. This lesson will be reinforced as more figures are considered.

In sum, subjects recognize Fig. 29 as a zebra, taking some segments of line as depictions of pigment borders. Lines can depict discontinuities of pigment.

Layout and Illumination

From surface layout and pigment layout we now turn to variation in illumination on surfaces and variation in illumination from surfaces—that is, shadows and highlights.

Shadows. When shadows are present on a surface, it is not uniformly illuminated. A shadow is cast on a surface when an opaque body is situated between a source of radiant light, or the direction of illumination, and the surface. The opaque body intercepts light that otherwise would reach the shadowed surface. Removing the opaque body allows the illumination to reach the surface. When an opaque body prevents illumination from reaching an area of a surface, the area is said to be cast in shadow.

Generally, terrestrial surfaces shadowed from the prevailing illumination are not entirely without illumination. Usually, light reflected from other objects and the sky reaches terrestrial areas shadowed from the sun. Thus, there is not the extreme contrast found with objects in empty space. Usually, too, terrestrial shadows result from objects intervening between surfaces and extended sources of illumination—not point sources. So there are penumbras to most shadows—regions where part of the extended source does offer illumination. Penumbras result in the softly blurred appearance of the margins of cast shadows.

Can cast shadows be depicted in outline? Outline drawings omit the brightness-darkness change entailed by shadows and the colors of shadows beloved of Impressionists. Outlines are made with fine, sharp lines and do not provide cross-hatching or other means to create gradients that would be like the gentle gradients in penumbras. These gradients seem important in recognition of shadow (Helmholtz, 1924; MacLeod, 1932). As a result, it may not be surprising that cast shadows are rare in outline drawings. In a sample of more than 10,000 line drawings from the Cornell Fine Arts Library, there were no examples of depictions of cast shadows. The majority of the drawings were recent European and American work, but collections from Japan, India and the Near East, and from Celtic and Anglo-Saxon times were included.

The rarity of outline representation of cast shadow suggested an experiment (Kennedy, 1970). Given this rarity, most subjects presumably have never been instructed that outlines can represent shadows. Would instruction be necessary for subjects to perceive shadows when shown (probably for the first time) an outline drawing in which cast shadows are represented?

To avoid problems with penumbras, photographs in which distant shadows were present were sought. Distant shadows can be far enough away that penumbra are not evident. For distant shadows, the angles subtended by the penumbra are so small that the transition between light and dark seems sharp to the unaided eye. Only photographs of terrestrial shadows were considered, those involving natural or ecological optics, not altered by darkroom or laboratory trickery such as reversing or altering illumination on the pictured scene with lenses or mirrors or artificial sources of light. In many of these photographs, shadows were easily recognized as such; thus, a penumbra is not necessary for a shadow to be recognized.

A particular line drawing (Fig. 30) was prepared from one of the photographs. The outline was made by "tracing" from selected portions of the picture. In particular, discontinuities of pigment representing shadows were traced from the photograph. In addition, human figures and luggage cases and a pole were depicted by lines in the drawing, traced from pigment arrangements in the photograph.

The photograph capitalizes on the laws of projection of light, and so it is in projective correspondence with an environment. The lines traced from the photograph are also in projective correspondence with features of the same environment. Can enough structure be retained in a projective line tracing to make the lines informative about corresponding features? In particular, will the pictured shadows be recognizable even to untrained observers?

FIGURE 30. An outline drawing depicting boundaries of shadows by lines.

Eight adult subjects—graduate psychology students at Cornell—were shown Fig. 30. They were asked, "What is this?"—nothing more direct. Six immediately identified the picture as depicting shadows. If the subject did not specifically say where the relevant lines were, and name the objects casting shadows, he was asked, "Shadows of what?" and "Which lines represent shadows?" The six subjects correctly identified the lines in the lower half of the figure as depictions of the shadows of men in a row, carrying flags.

Two subjects did not spontaneously identify the shadows. One said, "I don't know what this is" while indicating the lower half of the picture. The other said, "Is it water?" Both of these subjects were given a hint, the one word "Shadows." Both then correctly identified the shadows and correctly said what was casting the shadows. The hint did not indicate particular lines or suggest particular objects casting shadows. Still less was it instruction in a convention or an arbitrary code. The objects casting the shadows were not depicted in the drawing, so subjects could not identify an object and then guess, following the hint, that otherwise-meaningless scribbles "must be meant to be their shadows." Nor were there any flags or men standing in a row anywhere in the scene.

Perception of shadows in the drawing is not due to a learned convention. At the time, November 1969, there were few if any outline depictions of cast shadows on which a convention might have been based. Since 1969, examples have emerged in recent "revolutions" in graphic art, inspired by high-contrast photography (which emphasizes the structure of optic arrays, often at the expense of recognizability of the environmental source of the more demurely-contrasted array).

It seems that the capacity of outline to depict recognizable shadows is inherent in the perceptual skills of untrained adult observers. What were the important attributes of Fig. 30 that made it depict shadows rather than any of the host of other possibilities, from corners to color patches? Presumably, Fig. 30 must present aspects of shape that are distinctive to shadows.

What attributes does Fig. 30 have in common with shadows? The figure presents some of the shapes of men, but there are anomalies. Parts of the figures are surprisingly wide, and other parts in comparison are unusually narrow. The nearest arm of the shadow of the nearest man is a particularly clear case. Notice, too, that the wide parts point toward the observer, and thin parts are at right angles to these. And the shoulders of the figures are oddly skewed with respect to the main axis of the figures. Thus, the lower figures are projected as would be flat figures, not as voluminous solid objects. Their flat character distinguishes them from real men.

Also, there is no interior detail to the lower figures. The flags being carried are continuous with the standard and the standard with the human figures. Absence of internal detail is a common characteristic of shadows, particularly shadows in a natural scene with no artificial lighting. Further, the baggage, the pole, and the erect human figures define a ground plane and its horizon. These objects in these erect postures should be resting on a solid surface. The three human figures project smaller subtended angles, as their feet are depicted higher in the picture plane. The location of the feet and the decrease in size corresponding to height in the picture plane is perspective information for the location of a surface and its horizon. One could even work out what height the photographer held the camera, which would be the height at which the horizon intercepts the standing figures.

Just as the erect figures define a ground plane and an imaginary horizon, so, too, do the figures in the lower half of the illustration. The figures decrease in size and width as they move up the picture plane. The axes of the human figures and the standards converge toward the horizon; continued, they meet in one point. Thus, these flat figures provide perspective information for a surface and a horizon that corresponds to the surface defined by the erect figures. It is characteristic of cast shadows that they lie on surfaces, the very surfaces defined by other features of the environment.

Familiar figures that are present in outline, appearing flat, with no internal detail, merging smoothly with the shapes of other figures, lying on terrain without suggesting surfaces at variance with the rest of the environment—in such ways Fig. 30 contains information for shadows. Probably none of the subjects who identified shadows in the illumination could have identified many of the attributes of the outlines that specify shadows. The figures presumably capitalize on intuitive or tacit understanding of features of the visible world, just as in sound localization we can say where a sound source is but not how temporal differences at the ears are used to identify the location.

To support the analysis of the illustration of shadows, the figures were redrawn in various ways. The expectation was that if any attribute was altered, no observer would identify the result as a depiction of shadows. The attributes were divided into (a) those for flatness, (b) those for absence of internal detail, and (c) those for concurrence between the terrain and the surface bearing the flat figures. An illustration in which all three attributes have been altered is Fig. 31, which shows erect solid figures, men complete with internal detail. Compared to Fig. 30, attributes (a), (b), and (c) have been changed in Fig. 31. In Fig. 32, only (a) and (b) are changed.

Nine subjects (summer school students at Cornell) were shown Figs. 30, 31, and 32. They were simply asked to comment on the things pictured. Eight of the nine identified the shadows in Fig. 30. All nine identified the figures in Fig. 31 as being men standing in a row and did not mention shadows. No subject mentioned shadows for Fig. 32, seven of the subjects saying the figures were supine men. Two thought the men were strangely flattened—"cutouts," said one; "flattened," said the other.

When internal detail was added, but the flatness (or concurrence with a single plane) retained, subjects often commented on the flatness of the figures, saying for Fig. 33 that there was an impression of figures "painted on the ground" or "totally flat" or "flat and unreal." Again, no one mentioned shadows. However, when the internal detail was removed, as in Fig. 34, even if the outline was for a rounder, fuller figure, six out of nine subjects still mentioned shadows. The information for the solid silhouette of a man was not preventing subjects from using the lack of internal detail and location of the figures as information for a shadow.

Could the kind of difference between Fig. 30 and Fig. 34 be used by subjects? Perhaps the subjects were simply using lax criteria for form, assuming that the drawings are made roughly with no great emphasis on niceties of form. If so, subjects could be asked to compare two drawings including the kinds of difference distinguishing Fig. 30 and 34. Two extra drawings of vertical figures, different only in outline information for fullness or solidity (Fig. 35 and Fig. 36), were shown to all nine subjects. They were asked to say which looked more "bulky" and which looked more "flat." All nine subjects chose correctly—Fig. 35 was said to be more "bulky."

It seems that absence of internal detail, concurrence with surface, and flatness are distinguishing features of shadows. These aid subjects in recognizing outline depiction of shadows. Informa-

Fig. 31

Fig. 32

FIGURE 31.   The foreground figures are solid, detailed, and erect.

FIGURE 32.   The supine figures are solid and detailed.

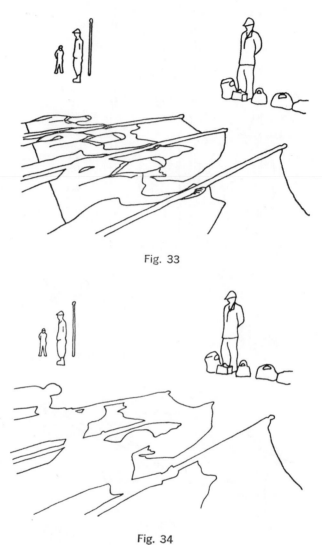

Fig. 33

Fig. 34

FIGURE 33.   The supine figures are flat and detailed.

FIGURE 34. The information for solidity—rather than flat shadows—
in the supine figures is often not detected.

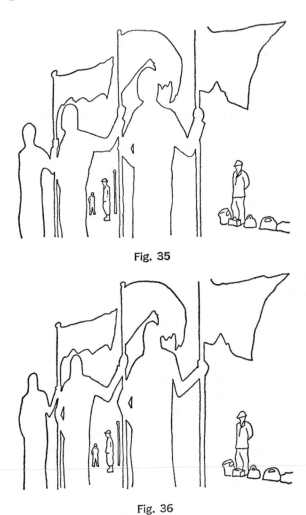

Fig. 35

Fig. 36

FIGURE 35.   The erect figures contain information for roundness or bulkiness.

FIGURE 36.   The erect figures contain information for flatness, unlike these in Figure 35.

tion for flatness may be the least helpful aid, if subjects are not discouraged from making allowances for imprecise drawing.

The general aim of the studies was fulfilled. They showed that outline can depict shadow, and shadows in outline depictions can be recognized without training in a convention.

Highlights. Shadows can be depicted in outlines. Can highlights, another phenomenon created by the relation of surface layout to illumination, also be shown in outline?

Highlights depend on surfaces being polished or smooth. Highlights appear when the relationship between three factors—a source of radiant light, a polished surface, and a point of observation—is just right. Shadows depend on surfaces and light sources and are independent of a point of observation; highlights are not. As an observer moves around, the surfaces showing highlights change. Just looking first with one eye and then with the other can produce remarkable changes in highlights.

In general, incident illumination is reflected off a surface either in a *specular* manner (mirror reflection off a smooth, polished surface) or by *scatter* reflection. If the surface is polished or smooth, illumination is reflected at an angle equal to its incident angle. In contrast, a rough surface scatters incident illumination in many directions. Often there is a compromise between scatter and specular reflection, and the surface is said to be partially polished.

If the surface is at all polished, a station point will receive particularly strong illumination from a direction meeting the surface at an angle equal to the incident angle of prevailing illumination (Fig. 37). Station point i in Fig. 37 receives light from points a and b on a surface, but the light from a is particularly intense. Station point i lies in a direction from a where incident illumination is being particularly strongly reflected. For station point ii, the illumination from b is particularly intense, for similar reasons. For station point i, there is a highlight in the direction of a. For station point ii, there is a highlight in the directon of b. If one eye were at i and the other at ii, the direction of a highlight would seem to shift from a to b, as an observer looked with one eye and then the other.

So discontinuities in optic arrays—discontinuities in the intensity of light from a surface to a station point—occur, given the right arrangements of sources of light, polished surfaces, and station points.

Are highlights recognizable in outline drawings? They are not uncommon in line drawings. Objects such as balloons and bottles, rounded, with smooth surfaces, are often drawn to include outline depiction of highlights (Fig. 38). Lines mark the margins of directions of discontinuities of illuminaton.

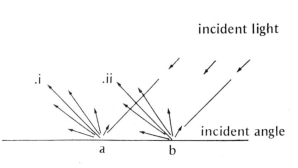

Length of these arrows indicates amount of light reflected in the direction of the arrows

incident light

Cross section of a partially polished surface

incident angle

Fig. 37

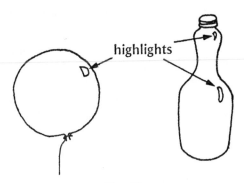

highlights

Fig. 38

FIGURE 37. If a surface is partially polished, most of the incident light is reflected at an angle equal to the incident angle.

FIGURE 38. Highlights on balloon and bottle.

Since outline depiction of highlights is fairly common, it is probably not necessary to test adults to see whether such outlines are recognizable, but it may be instructive to test children. My two child visitors (five and eight years old), mentioned previously, failed to identify the highlights depicted in Fig. 38. Asked what a highlight was, the younger was nonplussed. The older said, "Well, you take a light and put it up high!" Perhaps in that odd way that we can fail to notice our own shadow during the day, so children can fail to notice highlights until they are pointed out or become a source of play in a contemplative moment. At some point, tacit understanding is able to support outline depiction; the age at which that understanding is reached is still a matter for conjecture.

To summarize, line segments can depict discontinuities of illumination due to highlights or cast shadows, drawing on adult tacit understanding of the ecology of light.

Changes in Texture

A surface texture occurs when a unit is repeated over an area with stochastic regularity. A texture can be described in terms of the unit being repeated, the number of units in a given area, and the distribution of the unit. An arrangement of small areas of pigment may constitute a texture, as in a slab of speckled quartz. Small mounds and depressions may constitute a texture, as in ripples on a beach. Visible texture is created by arranging units defined by pigment or layout or illumination changes.

A discontinuity in texture occurs where a terrain abruptly changes its texture. On a beach, a pebbly area might adjoin an area of sand. A grassy area might change to lichen as underlying soils varied. As texture changed on a beach or area of vegetation, so, too, would color and general layout, in many cases. Finding a pure case of a texture change in nature is not easy.

Can a texture change be recognizably depicted by a line in an outline drawing? Since layout and pigment and illumination discontinuities can be depicted in outlines, it is necessary to find a pure case of texture change—one where no other kind of discontinuity is present. Otherwise, observers may recognize one kind of discontinuity being depicted and infer the other. So far I have discovered only one kind of pure texture change that is at all common; it is a kind found in garments. The hem of a sweater, for example, is often different from the body of the sweater, only in the arrangement of the strands that have been knit to form the sweater. The coloring is often identical in the body of the sweater and the hem. Except when the hem is folded up or rolled up, the surface layout remains at one level. The level of illumination from the sweater is the same from the body and hem. The distribution of tiny pockets of shadow, from the individual strands of the material, vary in the body and hem, creating a visible texture, but the general level of illumination remains the same. The discontinuity due to a hem is a pure case of a texture discontinuity.

Figure 39 is an outline drawing of a sweater, traced from a photograph, in which the junction of the hem with the body of the sweater is depicted by a line. No difference in coloring marks the boundary of the hem. Differences in weave are not indicated by differences in stippling or hatching. Is the line for the edge of the hem an effective depiction of a texture discontinuity, so that there is no need for captions or training in a convention? Consider replies from eight adult subjects (students at Cornell) asked about Fig. 39.

FIGURE 39. An outlined sweater, with line depiction of the upper border of a hem, to show change in texture.

The subjects were shown the drawing and asked nondirective questions. First they were asked, "What is this?", when the drawing was presented to them. They generally replied "Its a drawing of clothing—a sweater" or words to that effect. If the subject did not mention clothes—as in the case of one who said, "It looks like a page from *Sports Illustrated!*"—he was asked to say a little more. All subjects mentioned garments or sweaters specifically. The second question was about a specific line. The subject was asked,

"What is this?", as the experimenter pointed to the line depicting the outer edge (outer occluding bound) of the arm, just below the shoulder. All subjects identified the line correctly. They were then asked, "What is on this side of the line?", as the experimenter pointed to the interior of the represented arm. All subjects identified the area as the interior of the arm. They were then asked, "What is on this side?", and the experimenter pointed to the exterior region adjoining the line. Subjects said "Nothing" or "Air" or "Background" or words to that effect.

The next line they were asked about was the topmost horizontal line (for the neck) of the same sweater. Again the first question was, "What is this?", and the next two questions were, "What is on this side?", as the experimenter pointed to the two areas on either side of the line. All subjects mentioned the neck of the sweater and the neck of the wearer and mentioned the neck of the wearer was not specifically represented.

What these questions established was that subjects understood the questions despite their very general nature and that the picture depicted a sweater in the appropriate orientation to the subjects. Line depiction of layout was clearly effective for all these subjects. The line of questioning was clear and meaningful to all the subjects.

The next question centered on the line depicting the hem and was again nondirective. The experimenter pointed to the line that was a tracing of the upper boundary of the hem as shown in the original photograph. Subjects were asked, "What is this?" Six of the eight immediately mentioned a change of weave or knit or a change of pattern or said "It's the top of the hem" and, asked to enlarge, mentioned a change of weave. Of the other two subjects, one said "It could only be ribbing" and, questioned, explained that a rib was an elongated ridge knit into a sweater, and that the line in question represented a rib that ran parallel to the bottom edge of the sweater. The subject was adamant that ribbing was the only thing the line could represent. The other subject said that the line represented the join of the hem to the body of the sweater. This subject was unable to enlarge upon her answer, repeating, "the top of the hem" when asked to explain. Asked to explain further, she said she could not. Asked to explain what a hem was she could only say it was the bottom band of a sweater. It did not seem possible to have the subject use terms like texture (for example, "weave," "knit," "pattern," "matting," "braiding," "reticulation," "plaiting") without suggesting them directly, so the subject was not questioned further. Whether she was thinking of a hem in terms of weave but could not express this remains unsure.

So, six out of eight identified the line depiction of a texture discontinuity. What makes the line provide information about a texture change rather than any of the other things a line can depict? Why was it not the top of the rolled-up edge of the sweater? Presumably, the line pattern in the sketch must contain distinctive features of a texture change.

The figure provides a familiar configuration—a clothed body. The lines fit the overall shape of a human torso but also have characteristics of sweaters—curves representing folds, proportions that are bulkier than a nude body, and extra lines cutting across the limbs and body to depict cuffs for sleeves and the termination below the waist.

Consider the curves of lines that depict the sides of sleeves and the lower body of the sweater and the neck. The neck line changes direction; it swerves to show the silhouette of the bottom section of the folded-over roll neck. The cuff line swerves to indicate the end of the sleeve. These swerves depict layout edges—edges that can be silhouetted. Similarly, the bottom edge of the body of the sweater is marked by a line that comes down the side of the body and then swerves to become horizontal before it divides in two, a horizontal continuation and the vertical continuation. The lines for changes of layout swerve to silhouette each layout change. But lines for the side of the sweater do not swerve as they approach and form a junction with the line for the upper part of the hem. At that junction, the lines for the sides of the sweater continue undeviatingly. Accordingly, that line does not suggest a layout change.

The line for the texture discontinuity occurs in the midst of information for a garment and is parallel to and a short way above a line for a change of surface layout, the end of the material of the sweater. The line does not indicate a change of surface layout (like a line for the top of a belt, for example), since if it did, the line for the side of the body would change direction when close to it. The line is in the appropriate place for the border of a hem; such borders in sweaters are typically texture discontinuities.

Hems are sometimes marked by color change as well as texture change. Hems are not exclusively dependent on texture discontinuities. It is a little surprising that no subject mentioned a color change. Perhaps there is some feature of shape that distinguishes a pigment change from a texture change, and a drawing that includes such features would be a useful tool to explore the tacit knowledge underlying subjects' judgments.

In summary, subjects can recognize outline depiction of texture discontinuities, without training or captions. A drawing that subjects identify as depicting texture change by outline contains some distinguishing shape features of pure texture change.

Recognition of texture depiction by outline adds one more ecological phenomenon to a long list that can be identified in outline drawings.

Conclusion

Corners, whether convex or concave, occluding edges and occluding bounds, with or without backgrounds, parallel combinations of features of surface layout like wires or cracks, edges of shadows, highlights, and pigment boundaries—all yield to outline along with texture discontinuities. Perhaps *abrupt change* is the factor tying all these phenomena together. Abrupt change of depth or slant with respect to the station point is the result of a feature of surface layout. Abrupt change of illumination underlies shadows and highlights. Abrupt change of reflectance defines pigmentation change. And abrupt change in weave was depicted at the hem of a sweater.

The rule that follows is that lines can depict discontinuities, any of the visible discontinuities of surface, pigment, illumination, and texture layout. These are the basic features that create the visible environment. It follows that anything that has distinctive features of shape and is visible should be identifiable in outline drawings. The power of outlines does not rest on showing whole objects, which, of course, they can do, but on being able to present information for the fundamental features of the visible environment. The language of outline is a language of discontinuities and distinctive features of shapes. Cave artists mastered the vocabulary of surface layout, and still today that is the great domain of outline, the common pictorial language of many cultures. It seems other basic features of vision can be a part of that domain, too, when need arises.

In sum, outline drawings capitalize on ecological information provided by distinctive features of shape and permit observers without training or captions to identify basic discontinuities of shape, slant, pigment, illumination, and texture. Outline can depict discontinuities without reproducing the colors or textures or intensities that define each discontinuity, by presenting the informative variables of shapes that help distinguish each discontinuity.

Chapter Eight

Using the
Language of Lines

*T*o claim that light and pictures can be informative is not to deny that light and pictures can puzzle, too. In this chapter I will try to account for some of the puzzles and trickery in pictures. I will pry into ambiguity and into the workings of "reversible" displays, and I will try to explain "impossible" pictures yet show that the language of outlines is not violated by ambiguity, reversibility, and impossibility. Just as verbal language is systematic and yet capable of puzzling ambiguity, so is light and outline drawing.

Probing into the comparison between language and picturing, this chapter will consider whether the language of outline is restricted to vision. Experiments on touch with blind subjects will show what meanings outlines can have for the hand as well as the eye.

Ambiguity and Reversibility

Words and sentences can have many meanings. "Bow" can mean a ribbon, a part of a ship, or a posture. In "They are cooking apples," the word "cooking" can be a verb or an adjective. Similarly, an individual line can depict any of the basic features of the visible environment. Usually the pattern around the line determines what is referent is, just as the phrase around "bow" limits it to "the colorful bow in someone's hair," or "the proud bow of a courtier."

One can ask what meaning the word "bow" could have on its own. And, similarly, one can take a simple line pattern and ask what it could depict. A circle can depict a hoop, ball, or coin, a fact that suggests depiction is a matter of will and choice. But closer examination leads to a different conclusion. When a hoop is depicted, the line forming the circle depicts a wire. When a ball is depicted, the line depicts an occluding bound. To depict a coin, the line depicts the occluding edge of a disc. Notice that the referents are part of the language of outline.

A highly detailed drawing may be unambiguous in its referent, just as a full sentence around the word "bow" restricts the referent of the word. Ambiguity in perception results when only a few elements are considered, be they words or lines. And the perceiver then selects from a set of possible referents. In the case of language, the possible referents are an arbitrarily chosen set. In the case of lines, the referents are drawn from a language of outline depiction that is not arbitrary, for training is not necessary for recognition. It may be necessary to have some experience with detailed, high-fidelity pictures before one can treat simple drawings as pictures of many possible things; discovering ambiguities in figure-ground drawings is a skill that increases with age, and it is more developed in more intelligent children (Elkind and Scott, 1962). But the skill makes use of the language of outlines and does not introduce completely new referents. In this vein, consider the displays that demonstrate one-sided shaping effects.

At first, the incomplete letters in Fig. 40 are not seen. Shapes are visible, but not the shapes that could form parts of letters.

Meaningless blocks are seen at first. With a hint, one can reverse the figure. Then the lines no longer shape only the blocks; one notices the shapes on the other side of the lines. At first, the spaces between blocks seem like distant background behind occluding edges of surfaces. The enclosed areas seem like flat foreground surfaces, and the lines depict the edges of surfaces. When reversed, with letters visible, the lines still depict edges, but the flat foreground areas are now on the other side of the lines. In sum, the side where surface seems to be alternates in Fig. 40, yielding blocks or letters.

Another case of reversibility, one of the most famous, is Rubin's vase faces figure (Fig. 41). As a vase, the left and right lines represent rounded surfaces—that is, occluding bounds—with the bounded surface enclosed by the lines. The top line represents an occluding edge with surface below the line, and the bottom line depicts an occluding edge with surface above the line. As a face, each of the two sides again depict occluding bounds, but now they are occluding in the reverse direction. The top and bottom lines are irrelevant to the faces, and do not depict at all; that is, they are seen simply as lines on paper.

The figure-ground reversibility of Figs. 40 and 41 involves reversing the direction of occlusion. A circle depicting a disc at one moment and a window at the next involves the same kind of reversibility. However, if the circle depicts first a disc and then later a ball, it is not the direction of occlusion that changes. Instead, the line depicts first an occluding edge and later an occluding bound, a demonstration that reversals need not interchange figure and ground, the sides where shape is.

A beautiful example of a reversal that does not affect figure-ground is Fig. 42. At first the lines depict a billowing sail—and the sail may bow into the page or out of the page. With a switch of attention the lines can depict a kite, symmetrical about a diagonal axis. The figure is almost unrecognizably different as a sail and a kite, a reversal that is not figure-ground in type.

Yet another reversal, pointed out by Necker in 1832, is evident in depictions of wire objects or transparent objects. A Necker cube (Fig. 43) reverses so that its front face and its back face alternate. Its oblique lines *reorient* as the figure reverses. An-

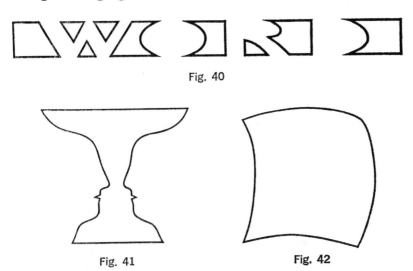

Fig. 40

Fig. 41   Fig. 42

FIGURE 40.   After a few moments, incomplete letters become visible.

FIGURE 41.   A figure can be seen as a vase or as two faces. This was used by Rubin to demonstrate figure-ground reversibility.

FIGURE 42.   The lines in this figure can be seen as depicting a billowing sail, or as a kite, symmetrical about a diagonal axis.

other figure giving rise to remarkable orientation reversals is a triangle like that in Fig. 44, which can be taken as a depiction of an isosceles triangle in depth. The orientation of the depicted triangle can be switched radically. The Necker cube is more complicated than the triangle. In the cube, there is change of occlusion as well as change of orientation. The wires "in front" where two lines cross usually switch as the obliques reorient. The "in front" changes reveal important aspects of depicting wires by lines. Usually, when a wire is depicted by a single line, features of wires are omitted, like information for their rounded cylindrical shape and their surface textures. (Similarly, the triangle is depicted without information for its orientation, and a circular line seen as a depiction of a hole does not provide information for the depth in the hole.) In some ways, the results of omission control Necker cube reversal. Where the wires overlap, it is not evident which line is "in front." But if

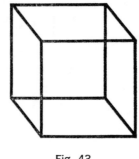

Fig. 43

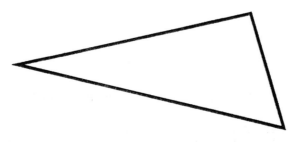

Fig. 44

FIGURE 43.   A Necker cube, which reverses so that the oblique lines reorient, and different lines appear to be to the front.

FIGURE 44.   This simple triangle can be seen oriented in the plane of the paper on which it is printed, or slanting first one way and then another.

the cube is redrawn (Fig. 45) as though made of thick wire, each side depicted by single lines, the cube is not so reversible. Information about which wire is in front is presented in Fig. 45. In general, the more information for which line is in front, the longer it will take for a wire cube to reverse (Howard, 1961).

It is not impossible to make Fig. 45 reverse. With a little effort, the left side can be seen depicting either a near face or a far face of the cube. After a little practice, odd mixtures of wires poking in different directions can be seen. Once Fig. 45 has been reversed, it can be reversed as readily as Fig. 43. Kennedy and Brust (1972) found that twelve-year-olds and adults (college students) reversed line-drawn cubes like those in Figs. 43 and 45 and three-dimensional cubes made of real wires at the same rate (about twenty-two times per minute in a period of two and a half minutes). Even making the front face a different color (black) than the back face (grey, as in Fig. 46) did not affect the rates of reversals. Similarly, Pandina, Zeller, and Lawson (1971) found a three-dimensional cube reversed as often as did a pictured cube. It seems that information for occlusion or depth is unimportant once reversals have begun. Only in the period before reversals have started—before the reversed appearance is discovered—is such information significant.

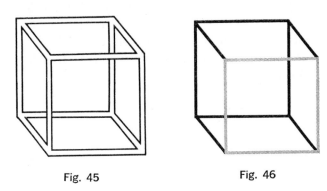

Fig. 45   Fig. 46

FIGURE 45. A cube drawn as though made of thick wire, each side of the wire depicted by a line, revealing clearly which faces of the cube are in front. With a little practice, even this cube can be reversed quite readily.

FIGURE 46. A wire cube made of wires of different shades.

Kennedy and Brust's finding makes sense if one thinks of reversals as involving a kind of attention, where the subject takes the display as depicting one thing and then another. Seeing something as a depiction involves a kind of attention, found in its purest form in looking at a simple figure like a circle and taking it to be a picture of a hoop. There is nothing about the circle that specifies a hoop rather than a hole, so it requires a special kind of pictorial attention to see the circle as a hoop depiction.

To suggest an attention mechanism here is to imply that the subject has two problems: first, he must discover what to attend to (the circle as a hole, or the reversed appearance of the Necker cube) and, second, he must reattend to what he has once dis-

covered. It is the first phase—discovery—that is influenced by information for depth and occlusion, in Necker cubes. The second
phase—reattending—is influenced only by the attention mechanism, and so is almost independent of the ecological information for
depth and occlusion.

Compare: In daily life we may not discover some aspect of
an object directly in front of us, but if the aspect is once discovered,
it is easy to attend to it again. (If one had to repeat the discovery
process, it would take as long again!) A useful case in point is an
incomplete picture, like that in Fig. 47. At first the lines seem
meaningless, but once an incomplete object has been found, the
object can be seen again at will. In Fig. 47 the original is a fork—
and once the incomplete fork is found, there is no trouble seeing it
a second time.

FIGURE 47.   An incomplete picture of a familiar object.

When a real wire cube is made to reverse, as the subjects in
Kennedy and Brust's study succeeded in doing, information for
depth and occlusion is being held in abeyance as irrelevant. Similarly, the flatness of the layout of lines in Fig. 42 is irrelevant to the
perception of a cube. The key skill in picture perception is to simultaneously notice the relevant and use the irrelevant only to avoid
trompe l'oeil. The Necker-cube studies suggest depth can be held in
abeyance with ease, by adults and twelve-year-olds, who see reversals at a constant rate despite the presence of stronger cues to depth.

Oddly enough, blasting the subject with sound, or confining
him in a super heated room, or strenuously exercising him increase
the rate of reversals of cubes (Vickers, 1972). Why these external
factors change the subjects' attention in a particular way is a mystery, but many factors can affect control over attention. Some factors should follow common sense. To speed the subject's perception
of a pictured object, ambiguity should probably be removed by the
addition of relevant details—otherwise, for instance, a circle meant

as a disc might be seen as a hole. Irrelevance should be kept to a minimum, otherwise the observer may overlook the relevant object. Not all the influences are so obvious, however. In the next section, I will consider some of the factors present in the picture.

Guiding Pictorial Perception

Understanding what is relevant and what is irrelevant in a picture is not always plain sailing. Some factors impede perception of others; some distortions do not mislead the observer.

In this light, let us reconsider the incomplete-fork picture (Fig. 47). One might conjecture that any form that had been altered would be recognized by a perceiver only if he could replace missing parts or (in general) reverse any alterations. Indeed, many authors have concluded that incomplete pictures call on the perceiver to set hypothetical completion processes into action, reversing the fragmentation that produced the incomplete picture. Street (1935) said that "in order to perceive the picture it is necessary to complete the structure, that is, to bring about a 'closure.' One of the requirements placed upon a subject is that in order to perceive the figure in its entirety, he supply, in his own mind at least, the missing parts." Leeper (1935) said of Street's displays "some figures . . . can be seen as pictures of certain familiar forms, provided you 'fill in,' as it were, the spaces between the fragments shown."

Taken literally, Street and Leeper are suggesting that one's seeing Fig. 47 as a fork produces an impression that some extra lines are added or filled in. But, of course, the figure does not seem to suddenly acquire new lines when the identity of the represented object becomes apparent. A more acceptable explanation is that incomplete pictures like that in Fig. 47 are difficult to identify because of special problems in distinguishing relevant features from irrelevant rubble. Note that when Fig. 47 was made incomplete, extra lines not relevant to the fork were added. If the relevant and irrelevant lines are clearly distinguished, as in Fig. 48, the fork becomes much easier to identify, without any more relevant information being added (Kennedy, 1971). It is easier to separate the relevant from the irrelevant in Fig. 48.

FIGURE 48. Lines that are relevant to a fork are distinguished from the other lines in this figure. Even though no additional lines for the fork have been added, the fork is more readily seen in this figure than in Figure 47.

What guides the perceiver in deciding what is relevant and what is irrelevant? The influences—from habit and stylistic canons to instructions, keys, and captions—vary. In a sense, the flatness of the surface of a picture is always irrelevant to what is depicted, but even the flatness may play some mysterious roles. For example, Pirenne (1970) has suggested ways in which an awareness of the surface of the picture may aid picture perception.

Pirenne noted that pictures are surprisingly unaffected by being viewed from awkward angles. Consider viewing a photograph from directly in front and from an awkward side angle. Imagine the central patch in the photograph is a circle—say, a globe of the world depicted by a circular form. To the front, the circle casts a symmetrical cone of light. To the side it casts an elliptical cone of light. Pirenne notes that the depicted globe still looks spherical when viewed from the side. Somehow, vision can accommodate for askew observation angles and the change of forms in the light to various viewing positions. Pirenne theorizes that the eye takes into account the information for the surface of the picture and computes the shape of the forms on the surface. The observer becomes aware of the depicting forms and thus of the depicted forms. Viewing from any angle, the observer realizes that the form on the picture surface is a circle and takes a circle as a depiction of a sphere.

Pirenne's theory makes appealing use of an awareness of the physical reality of the picture, a reality that is overlooked only in *trompe l'oeil*. But the theory has an Achilles' heel. Imagine again viewing the photograph from directly in front. But suppose two spheres are depicted, one in the middle of the picture and one off to the side, both projecting symmetrical cones of light to the eye. Now, if the eye were to compute the shapes of the patches on the surface, one patch would be circular and the other would be elliptical. Pirenne's theory would predict that only the circular patch would allow the observer to see a sphere depicted. But Pirenne finds that both the elliptical and the circular patches give the impression of a spherical object. As a result, a theory meant to explain correct perception despite awkward viewing angles cannot predict the perception that occurs from simple, direct viewing positions.

With Pirenne, we may conclude that an awareness of the surface is important to avoid *trompe l'oeil,* if nothing else. But the details of how that awareness guides us in perceiving forms remains an open question.

Differences in elements can speed recognition of an incomplete figure. Surface perception may aid perception from indirect viewing angles. Also, the overall pattern in the display must aid the observer in identifying what is depicted by particular elements, otherwise any element would be ambiguous. In some cases, the overall pattern can act like sleight of hand, making the elements almost undetectable. This lesson is often emphasized by Gestalt psychologists, and it is particularly relevant to outline depiction.

Consider Fig. 49. This figure is usually seen as a hand or glove with fingers outstretched and touching one another all along the sides. The drawing is an outline drawing, and so there are two contours, one for each side of the line. Since the figure is closed—it completely surrounds the enclosed area—there is an inner contour and an outer contour. The outer contour has exactly the same shape as the contour shown in Fig. 50. The inner contour has exactly the same shape as the contour shown in Fig. 51.

Fig. 50 shows a mitten, with bulges for the tips of fingers. Fig. 51 shows a glove with its fingers separated. So Fig. 49 depicts a glove, fingers together, but neither of the contours of its line depict a glove, fingers together.

Fig. 49 contains the contours shown in Figs. 50 and 51, but no one normally sees the shapes depicted by these contours. That is, the line figure does not depict the sum of the things depicted by its contours! One sees the structure of the line figure, not structures made by its elements.

The glove and mitten fingers are not reversible like Necker

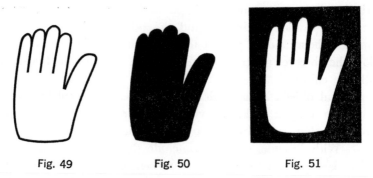

Fig. 49   Fig. 50   Fig. 51

FIGURE 49.   A gloved hand, fingers touching one another.

FIGURE 50.   A mittened hand, its fingers not discernible.

FIGURE 51.   A gloved hand, its fingers separated, not touching one another.

cubes or figure-ground displays, for they do not fluctuate between different incompatible states. They are not incomplete, for nothing is subtracted in making Fig. 49 out of Fig. 50 and Fig. 51. The figures are of a special type that reveals the contrast between line and its contours (Kennedy, 1972). The overall line structure "sleights" the shapes of the contours; by sleight of drawing, the contours are buried invisibly in the overall pattern.

In "sleighting" figures, the elements are overshadowed by the overall pattern; their relevance is to the production of the over-all impression, not as shapes in their own right. In caricatures, comparable results are produced. There are many relations between forms in caricatures that are there for effect rather than for accurate depiction. Do caricatures therefore make the depicted object less obvious? Do caricatures mislead the eye?

Caricatures. One might think that the most easily understood picture of an object should be in strict geometric correspondence with the object. But this is not so, for in some cases departure from fidelity seems to aid perception.

Ryan and Schwartz (1956) made different kinds of pictures of the same objects: black-and-white photographs, ink-and-wash drawings (drawings with shading), outline drawings, and cartoon drawings (that is, caricatures). Individual pictures were exposed for short periods, in a tachistoscope, and subjects had to report the positions of parts of the objects—for example, the posture of fingers when a hand was depicted, or the positions of switches when electrical controls were shown. In the caricature drawings, a hand had a thumb and three fingers, like that of a Disney character, and the digits were drawn with smooth curves, omitting details such as knuckles and wrinkles (cartoon conventions, these are called).

Ryan and Schwartz found the caricatures needed less exposure time than any of the other kinds of pictures. The photographs and shaded drawings were about equal. The high-fidelity line drawings needed the longest times. So, some distortions—ones used in caricatures and cartoons—can aid perception more than strict adherance to geometrical fidelity.

Ryan and Schwartz found that perception was speeded by caricature. Perkins (1970, personal communication) found caricatures to be especially accurate for recognition. Perkins had subjects trace photographs of well-known people—politicians, especially. The drawings the subjects made were mostly unrecognizable. Then Perkins told his subjects to exaggerate features of the sitter: if the politician's nose was large, in the drawing it should be made enormous; if the hairline receded, the drawing should show it as being even higher. The second set of drawings—besides being more entertaining to make and look at—were much more recognizable than the first.

In like vein, Dwyer (1967) found that realistic photographs of organs added nothing to students' understanding of a medical lecture, whereas cartoon drawings of the same organs contributed significantly. (In Dwyer's study, shaded line drawings were as effective as the cartoon. Perhaps sensitive measurements would have proved the superiority of the cartoons demonstrated by Perkins and by Ryan and Schwartz.)

Caricature is to drawing what hyperbole is to language. "A real man, as big as a mountain" may be a fitting description; despite exaggeration, meaning is conveyed. Exact size is distorted, but the remarkable size is not. A caricature may suggest sharp eyes like a rat's; the exact features of the person caricatured are distorted, but aspects of the features are displayed accurately. We are not misled by the caricature, any more than we are by hyperbole. Indeed, it just might be that mundane, high-fidelity passport photos may mislead us more and tell us less than would a good caricature—that is what the research suggests!

Impossibles. There is another parallel to be drawn between language and depiction. Combining incompatible words makes an "impossible" sentence, a sentence that can have no direct referent in reality. An example is "Colorless green ideas sleep furiously." The sentence is grammatical—it is not nonsense like "furiously sleep ideas green colorless." A drawing, too, can show impossible things, things that cannot have a direct equivalent in reality. Fig. 52 shows an impossible object, affectionately known as the Devil's tuning fork.

The reason for the fork's impossibility is that it combines features in incompatible ways, many authors have pointed out. What is the root of the impossibility? It is sometimes said that the flaw in the fork is the combination of depth cues. Perhaps that is misleading, for the fork could not be made of flat sheets of card or metal, all in one depth plane, as I will show. It is sometimes said that the flaw is that "the middle prong appears in two places at the same time . . . [but] one part of an object cannot exist in two places at the same time. The middle prong cannot both be at the *same* depth as the outer two and [be] *below* them" (Gregory, 1970, p. 57). That, too, is misleading. First, a middle prong could *slant down* to be below an outer prong at one end and above an outer prong at another end. Second, there simply is no evidence for one part of the middle prong being in two places at the same time. The figure looks uncertain, and parts of it reverse occasionally—but reversibility is not impossibility or being in two places at the same time.

Another possible explanation of the fork's impossibility is that there are two limbs at one end and three at the other. That is not the key either, for limbs can bifurcate, like the limbs of a tree, so one can start one end with two limbs and have as many as he liked at the other end.

There is no paradox in the lines themselves; the fact that they are on paper before us shows that. Paradox can only arise when the lines are taken as something else—that is, seen as picturing boundaries of surfaces. A line-by-line check should show how the fork violates rules governing boundaries of surfaces. That is, if nature arranges solid surfaces and intervening air spaces in only a few ways, it should be possible to show that the fork abuses those ways.

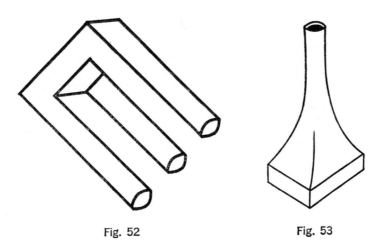

Fig. 52   Fig. 53

FIGURE 52.   An impossible object known as the Devil's tuning fork.

FIGURE 53.   A candlestick, round at the top, square at the base, whose outermost edges begin as sharp and, as the stick tapers, become rounded.

The outermost lines of the limbs begin by representing occluding edges and finish by depicting occluding bounds. Does that violate nature? The answer is no. As Fig. 53 shows, a line can depict an occluding bound at one end and an occluding edge at the other to show an object like a candlestick, round at the top and square at the base. The lesson is that some changes of representation along the length of a continuous line are quite acceptable. If the outline is to seem paradoxical, it is the kind of change—not change itself—that must be the flaw.

In the Devil's tuning fork, the first pair of lines in from the outermost show at one end a convex corner, made by the two sides of the square limbs. At the other end they depict occluding bounds;

with surfaces on one side and air space in between. Here is the heart of the paradox. In a violation of nature, what was surface has become air space. Similarly, the innermost lines depict occluding bounds at one end (enclosing surface) and occluding bounds at the other end (enclosing air space). The direction of occlusion has reversed, from one end of the line to the other, so that surface and air space have interchanged.

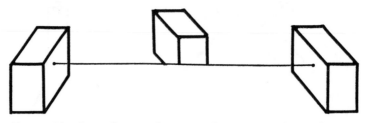

FIGURE 54. In reality, a wire cannot become an edge, as it does here.

The fork is impossible because of the kinds of changes depicted. What is impossible is that a boundary between surface and air should reverse so that air is on the same side of a boundary as a surface. The direction of occlusion, in nature, cannot reverse as it does in the innermost pair of lines of the fork, and occlusion cannot appear where previously there was a convex corner, as in the middle pair of lines.

Similarly, a wire (air on both sides) cannot turn into an occluding edge (air on one side), as in Fig. 54. Surface cannot simply cease to exist, as it does in Fig. 55 (after Josef Albers). Nor can a crack (surface on both sides) turn into edges or wires (air on one or both sides), as in Fig. 56 (after Lochlan Magee). None of these paradoxical figures could be cut from flat sheets (solid surfaces), for the rules of solidity are violated, though all of these figures can be drawn with lines or made from wires. It is as depictions of surfaces with edges that they show impossible objects. In language, the rule sounds as implausible as the objects look—"passing from surface to air we find ourselves passing from air to surface."

In impossibles, each part is ecological, but the combination of the parts violates nature. They could not exist, so they are imaginary, but the fact that they are imaginary does not make them im-

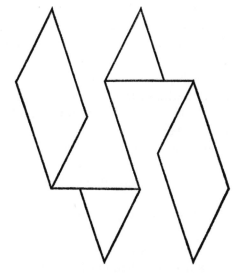

Fig. 55

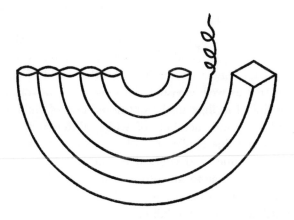

Fig. 56

FIGURE 55. In this anomalous drawing, surfaces are initiated but not terminated.

FIGURE 56. In reality, a crack cannot become an edge or a wire, as here.

possible. To make an imaginary object, parts are combined in possible ways. The combination can be possible but be a combination that does not exist. For example, there is nothing about surfaces and air spaces that rules out a horse with a horn, like a unicorn. Nature has not seen fit to evolve unicorns, but it could do so without contravening its own ways with surfaces and air. The parts of a unicorn are ecological. The combination of parts breaks no laws of solidity. In language, one may claim "I saw a unicorn, a horse with a horn." In language, as in pictures, to be imaginative is to combine familiar parts in possible but novel ways, whereas to be impossible is to combine the parts in novel ways that violate rules of nature.

Depiction Without Vision

At first thought, picturing may seem inherently something for the eye and language may seem much freer than depiction. Language comes spoken, written, semaphored, or tapped in Morse. Language seems above and beyond any one sense. Must picturing be locked in one modality, owned solely by vision?

Many of the things found depicted in visual displays are not inherently visual. Space and form are not inherently visual. The geometry of edges and surrounding air—the world of corners and wires—is tactual as well as visual. This geometrical world, research indicates, is linked to lines in the untutored eyes of children, people of other cultures, and members of widely different species, all of whom understand line depiction with little or no training. Perhaps the link between lines and edges does not only belong to the eye, but goes beyond vision to an intuitive understanding of form and structure that belongs to many senses; it is amodal in the sense that it is not restricted to one modality.

That the link between objects and pictures is far from the eye is suggested by research reported by White *et al.* (1969), who found that skin (on the back) can act as a kind of retina. White *et al.* used a television apparatus to press silhouettes of objects onto backs of blind and sighted subjects. With a little practice, subjects could identify the silhouettes. To some extent, this may be simply the identification of an object physically pressed on one's skin, which is not a pictorial task. But there are some suggestions in White's work that genuine pictorial skills were involved. For example, sometimes an expanding silhouette was "felt" as an object receding. Shrinkage felt like distance, not diminution. So, features of the flat array on the back were understood as representing features of a three-dimensional world.

If the flat displays show objects with overlap (occlusion) present, not simply silhouettes, and are drawn as lines flat on a sheet, then pictorial skills are necessary for one to identify the objects. The lines would have to be understood as representing boundaries of surfaces, sometimes with occluded background. Accordingly, Kennedy and Fox (in press) attempted to establish whether there is an untutored link between solid objects and flat outlines for blind subjects. Eight blind subjects were asked to explore raised lines with their fingers. The subjects were told that the displays—shown in Figs. 57 and 58—represented objects or parts of objects. The displays were pretested on thirty-four sighted subjects, all of whom recognized the displays correctly at first glance. The task, the blind subjects were told, was to identify the pictured object within two minutes.

The blind subjects had never used line drawings of objects before, they said. All used braille or readers as sources of information. All were at college, and were between eighteen and twenty-four years old. With one exception, they all had been blind since birth or within a few months of birth. The exception had lost his sight at the age of six.

Was the task meaningless to the subjects? The extreme hypothesis that all pictures are conventions predicts that the subjects would be totally lost. Being asked to compare lines with real objects should be as meaningless as comparing octopi and paychecks, if only a convention ties the two together.

Were any displays identified? Which should be more difficult? One might expect flattish objects to be easiest to identify—that is, objects that can make a recognizable imprint on a flat surface because they have little depth or overlapping parts. So the fork, hand, flag, and man with upraised arm should be easier than three-dimensional figures like the three-quarter-view face, the table, the man with his arms crossed, and the cup. The three-dimensional figures have overlapping parts and result in projective distortions—

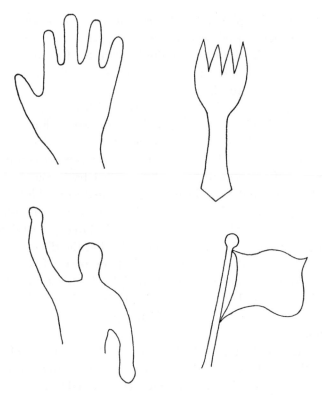

FIGURE 57. Figures not containing overlap or projective distortions ("imprints"). These figures were drawn as raised lines on plastic sheets and were explored by touch by blind and blindfolded subjects.

like a circular cup projecting an elliptical brim and a table projecting a parallelogram. If occluding edges and bounds, with background, mean little to the blind, projections should be difficult to identify.

Some subjects did not identify any of the eight displays, and some identified half. Two of the subjects identified four displays each (five each, if calling a cup a "container" or first labeling the fork correctly, and then retracting the name, are considered acceptable). Two identified one display each. Four identified no displays.

The occasional successes suggest some untutored links between lines and solid forms, in touch. The displays that were recognized included the hand (three times), the fork (twice), the cup

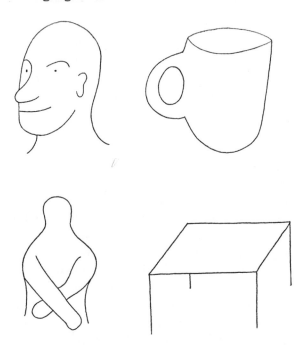

FIGURE 58. Figures containing overlap or projective distortions ("projections"), drawn as raised lines on plastic sheets.

(twice), the table (twice), and the face (once). Interestingly, there is no hint that plane imprints are easier than projective forms, for an equal number of imprints and projections were identified (five each). In later testing, four high-school blind subjects identified two or three displays each, usually the cup, table, and hand, but once including the flag and once including the man with his arms crossed. Evidently, lines depicting boundaries of surfaces, sometimes with background behind occluding edges and bounds, seem appropriate to some blind subjects.

The failure to pick out the correct label for the form does not mean the lines are meaningless, for the kinds of errors subjects made were curiously appropriate. Subjects misidentified the fork as an arm and a hand, which almost fits the display to vision. Equally reasonable to vision was misidentifying the fork as a tulip with a thick stem, as "an ice-cream cone with an unusual bottom," or as a bell on a kind of chain. Similarly reasonable are misidentification of the table as a house with a slanted roof or the man with upraised arm as a kind of teapot. Each of these errors makes pictorial sense to vision, suggesting new, appropriate ways of seeing the figures. The line marking the interior of the handle of the cup bothered some subjects, who took the line to be a solid form rather than a hole; again this is an appropriate error, suggesting figure-ground effects in touch.

At the end of testing, subjects were told the correct referents for each display. In most cases, the picture was then understood; given just the label (for example, "a cup") the subjects could pick out the parts, proving they did understand. At this point too, subjects were sometimes able to comment on how to make the displays more identifiable. Two said the reason the fork was difficult was trivial—the prongs were too close to be readily distinguished by touch. One said the man with his arms crossed was too round shouldered, which is visibly true, too, though sighted subjects usually do not notice how exaggerated the roundness is. Three said that a line was missing on the cup, that there should be a line marking where the handle joins the body of the cup.

The number of correct identifications is impressive on its own. But the numerical data is only the tip of iceberg of consistent comments and suggestions. The blind subjects found the idea of line depiction meaningful, could identify outline depictions without hints, could identify the parts of depictions given one-word hints, and could suggest uses of line in keeping with the use of outline in vision. There seems to be some deeply rooted human capacity to understand outline depiction of features of solid objects, a capacity that applies the same rules to vision and to touch. A box of brain cells, as it were, out of the visual pathways and out of the touch pathways but with access to vision and touch, deals with discontinuities in either vision or touch and accepts lines as equivalents of the discontinuities.

Conclusion

Outlines are useful for presenting essential details with a minimum of irrelevancy. In an outline drawing, key facts about the sizes, shapes, and locations of objects can be shown in a form of representation that requires less training than any code or language, less time than listening to a description, and little if any translation for its message to be universally understood. Outline pictures are representations—calling on a basic understanding of the nature of signs. Like language, they make use of meaningless units, for as outline pictures have their simple strips of line, so language has its phonemes. Both outline pictures and language put together their basic units to form meaningful packages (patterns and sentences). Accordingly, they should have much in common and this chapter has described the similar roles played by ambiguity and impossibility in both language and depiction, and shown how hyperbole and caricature have allied effects.

Language is meaningful to many modalities, many of our sensory systems. Looking for comparable properties of pictures, this chapter has presented research on pictures for blind people.

Picturing seems to be a form of communication meaningful to both vision and touch, without tuition. Picturing was discovered by early men, not invented and passed on by careful inculcation. To make pictures is an art, but recognition of depictions is largely a gift the environment and nature allows us gratis. In discovering outline picturing, early man capitalized on a capacity that is present because of an intuitive, amodal understanding of line and form, a capacity usually invoked visually, but with a potential for untutored touch.

Epilogue

*T*o do justice to the perception of objects represented in pictures requires some philosophy, some physics, and some psychology. Let me now briefly retrace my steps through these disciplines. The problem I have examined is how to identify the skills involved in seeing the form and location of objects and their parts. If vision is to be accurate, it must have optical information available to it. That information, in turn, depends on the laws of light. The place in which those laws operate is the environment of the perceiver. Thus, the task of the perceiver can be fully understood only if his tools are clearly known.

Accordingly, to introduce the tasks of the perceiver, I began by asking about information. The first chapter, the first step in my argument, described the kind of perception to be discussed, and some kinds of experiences and impressions perception permits us. A theory about everyday perception and its accuracy—a registration theory—was briefly proposed, and compared to a contrasting theory—a constructive theory. If everyday perception is to be accurate, it needs to rely on precise and unambiguous information, it was proposed. Therefore the role of optic information and the conditions under which light can be unambiguous had to be examined.

The second step of the argument was an analysis of the

156

everyday environment, its objects and surfaces, its points of observation and its medium for transmitting light. Light in the form of an optic array—an array at a point of observation—could be informative, it was proposed, if features of the array could only originate in particular ecological conditions. At this juncture, the puzzle of representation was noted. Light can come from a picture of an object or from the solid object itself. How then can light be unambiguous? To resolve the puzzle, it was proposed that the laws of information in light should be established with a natural environment, a world of regularly textured surfaces, innocent of artificial intervention.

Once the natural environment is described, the effects of manufacturing pictures—indeed, the possibility that pictures can be made at all—can be made to fit consistently into our understanding of light and perception. Pictures, latecomers to the world, can capitalize on pre-established laws. The laws of information in an apictorial world are manipulated by picture makers for representational effects.

The next step in the argument involved testing the optical-information definition of a picture. Contrasting definitions were offered, and their merits weighed. At least one contrasting definition made logical sense, and could be tested empirically. That contrasting theory conjectured that pictures belong to a system of arbitrary conventions, learned much as one learns to read alphabetic writing. This theory predicts that pictures will not have the same significance in different cultures, or to different species, that they will be meaningless daubs to any child who has not been schooled in their conventions, and that they will not trick the eye into believing the depicted object is real. In fact, a survey of research showed that most of the evidence contradicts these predictions, and supports the optical information theory.

The convention theory is not without merit, because many pictures are ambiguous, and many simple line drawings, which do not provide specific information for particular objects, can be seen in many ways. This fact was treated with great care in a judicious step in the argument, where the nature of figure, ground, and reversible line and contour patterns was analyzed. Though a generation of research has taken figure and ground to be an inevitable result of the perception of lines and contours, it was proposed that the originator of the concepts, Edgar Rubin, had been misunderstood. Then, though Rubin's description of the effects of looking at lines and contours was championed, his interpretation was challenged. Rubin saw a mosaic of different shape and depth effects, all of which seem to follow inexorably from the special skill of taking a line or contour as a pictorial device. As the key to this new interpretation, it was noted that Rubin neglected to consider the fact that his mosaic of effects included the way in which one can tell that none of these effects is physically true—one can distinguish what is truly before one's eyes and what is only apparent, what is perception and what is pictorial perception.

Following this re-interpretation, acknowledging J. J. Gibson's lead, the next step was to uncover the language or range of outline depiction. The elements of the visible environment were defined, and the kinds of patterns that specify them were presented. Features of layout of surfaces, of change of color, and of variation in illumination and texture were presented in outline, pictorial form. The powers of outline depiction seemed best summarized in the phrase "lines can depict visible discontinuities."

Lines being ambiguous elements, they need to be embedded in a pattern to have specific significance. This much pictures have in common with language. While language is founded on conventions of reference and pictures are founded in optical information, both manipulate elements into larger units—patterns and sentences—to make them specific to a given referent. Thus, the final step in the argument was able to draw parallels between these two modes of representation. The ambiguity of a word is comparable to the ambiguity of a simple line pattern, though words can have reference by convention and lines can only select from circumscribed sets of features that can be depicted. In both language and pictures, impossible things can be made known—as the sentence "colorless green ideas sleep furiously" suggests an impossible event. Hyperbole is useful in language, and in a similar vein caricature is useful in depiction. In a most interesting finding, the cross-modal significance of language was matched in research on untrained blind subjects.

Where may the argument be taken next? In some research with Lochlan Magee I am testing procedures for discovering the content of a picture. Strategies of search are given to subjects, who either follow the strategy at their own pace or are passively taken through the strategy under the control of the experimenter. We find that the active self-paced subjects discover less about some pictures than the guided, passive subjects. We are puzzled by this result, and are continuing to investigate it.

Another line of investigation has taken Judy Silver and myself toward the cave paintings of four continents, trying to establish the common language of outline depiction manifested in antipodal regions of the primitive world. We find that much of the language or range of outlining described in Chapter Seven was evident in the earliest and most widespread artifacts of man.

Research on children and adults, on *trompe l'oeil* and the skill in distinguishing what is real and what is apparent, has been a continuing preoccupation. Lochlan Magee, for example, has confirmed the deceptive quality of outlined objects seen on the periphery of vision, described in Chapter Four. In working with an eight-year-old I was fascinated to have him begin by being unable to see some of the subjective effects allowed by line displays, and then slowly discover them. He reported the real lines that were physically present, then noticed a shaping effect he had been unable to perceive at first, and then he reported with great interest that he could see the shape of this "funny" line change as he watched it.

With Abraham Ross I am planning some research on pictures to be attempted in New Guinea. We would like to check each of the claims made in Chapter Seven. With Laura Johnson I am planning to investigate the educational practices of different cultures, to see how different cultures introduce pictures to children.

Many disciplines have found their place in this discussion. Perhaps many more will be touched in the next few years, if the discussion stimulates the community of scholars and disciplines.

To close, let me simply say that pictures work because light is informative, pictures make use of the laws of naturalistic light, and pictures can play with light and perception to afford us impossibility, ambiguity, and caricature as well as faithful information.

References

ARNHEIM, R. "The Gestalt Theory of Expression." *Psychological Review*, 1949, *56*, 156–171.

ARNHEIM, R. *Art and Visual Perception*. Berkeley and Los Angeles: University of California Press, 1954.

ARNHEIM, R. *Toward a Psychology of Art*. Berkeley and Los Angeles: University of California Press, 1966.

BECK, J. "Perceptual Grouping Produced by Line Figures." *Perception and Psychophysics*, 1966, *1*, 300–302.

BERLYNE, D. E. "Ends and Means of Experimental Aesthetics." *Canadian Journal of Psychology*, 1972, *26*, 303–325.

BERNHEIMER, R. *The Nature of Representation*. New York: New York University Press, 1961.

BIEUSHEUVEL, S. "Psychological Tests and Their Application to Non-European Peoples." In G. B. Jeffrey (Ed.), *Yearbook of Education*. London: University of London Press, 1947.

BOND, E. K. "Perception of Form by the Human Infant." *Psychological Bulletin*, 1972, *77*, 225–245.

BOTHA, E. "Practice Without Reward and Figure-Ground Perceptions of Adults and Children." *Perceptual and Motor Skills*, 1963, *16*, 271–273.

BOWER, T. G. R. "Discrimination of Depth in Premotor Infants." *Psychonomic Science*, 1964, *1*, 368.

BOWER, T. G. R. "Stimulus Variables Determining Space Perception." *Science*, 1965, *149*, 88–89.

161

BOWER, T. G. R. "Slant Perception and Shape Constancy in Infants." *Science,* 1966, *151,* 832–834.

BOWER, T. G. R. "The Object in the World of the Infant." *Scientific American,* 1971, *225,* 30–38.

BOWER, T. G. R. "Object Perception in Infants." *Perception,* 1972, *1,* 15–30.

BRAUNSTEIN, M. L. "Motion and Texture as Sources of Slant Information." *Journal of Experimental Psychology,* 1968, *78,* 247–253.

BRODATZ, P. *Textures.* New York: Dover, 1966.

DAVENPORT, R. K., and ROGERS, C. M. "Perception of Photographs by Apes." *Behavior,* 1971, *39,* 318–320.

DAWSON, J. L. M. "Cultural and Physiological Influence on Spatial-Perceptual Processes in West Africa." *International Journal of Psychology,* 1967, *2,* Part I, 115–128; Part II, 171–185.

DENNIS, W. "The Human Figure Drawings of Bedouins." *Journal of Social Psychology,* 1960, *52,* 209–219.

DEREGOWSKI, J. B. "Picture Recognition in Subjects from a Relatively Pictureless Environment." *African Social Research,* 1968a, *5,* 356–364.

DEREGOWSKI, J. B. "Difficulties in Pictorial Depth Perception in Africa." *British Journal of Psychology,* 1968b, *59,* 195–204.

DEREGOWSKI, J. B. "A Note on the Possible Determinant of Split-Representation as an Artistic Style." *International Journal of Psychology,* 1970, *5,* 21–26.

DWYER, F. M., JR. "Adapting Visual Illustrations for Effective Learning." *Harvard Educational Review,* 1967, *37,* 250–263.

ELKIND, D. "Developmental Studies of Figurative Perception." *Advances in Child Behavior and Development,* 1970, *4,* 2–29.

ELKIND, D., and SCOTT, L. "Studies in Perceptual Development. I. The Decentering of Perception." *Child Development,* 1962, *33,* 1153–1161.

EPSTEIN, W. *Varieties of Perceptual Learning.* New York: McGraw-Hill, 1967.

FREEMAN, R. B., JR. "Ecological Optics and Visual Slant." *Psychological Review,* 1965, *72,* 501–504.

GARDNER, H. *The Arts and Human Development.* New York: Wiley, 1973.

GELDARD, F. A. *Fundamentals of Psychology.* New York: Wiley, 1962.

GIBSON, E. J. *Principles of Perceptual Learning and Development.* New York: Appleton-Century-Crofts, 1969.

References 163

GIBSON, J .J. *The Perception of the Visual World*. Boston: Houghton Mifflin, 1950.

GIBSON, J. J. "What Is a Form?" *Psychological Review*, 1951, *58*, 403–412.

GIBSON, J. J. "A Theory of Pictorial Perception." *Audio-Visual Communication Review*, 1954, *1*, 3–23.

GIBSON, J. J. "The Nonprojective Aspects of the Rorschach Experiments. IV. The Rorschach Blots Considered as Pictures." *Journal of Social Psychology*, 1956, *44*, 203–206.

GIBSON, J. J. "Pictures, Perspective, and Perception." *Daedalus*, 1960, *89*, 216–227.

GIBSON, J. J. *The Senses Considered as Perceptual Systems*. Boston: Houghton Mifflin, 1966.

GIBSON, J. J. "The Legacies of Koffka's *Principles*." American Psychological Association Conference, 1969.

GIBSON, J .J. "The Information Available in Pictures." *Leonardo*, 1971, *4*, 27–35.

GIBSON, J. J., and GIBSON, E. J. "Perceptual Learning: Differentiation or Enrichment?" *Psychological Review*, 1955, *62*, 32–41.

GOLLIN, E. S. "Developmental Studies of Visual Recognition of Incomplete Objects." *Perceptual and Motor Skills*, 1960, *11*, 289–298.

GOLLIN, E. S. "Further Studies of Visual Recognition of Incomplete Objects." *Perceptual and Motor Skills*, 1961, *13*, 307–314.

GOMBRICH, E. H. *Art and Illusion*, 2nd ed. Princeton, N.J.: Princeton University Press, 1961.

GOMBRICH, E. H. "The 'What' and the 'How': Perspective Representation and the Phenomenal World." In R. Rudner and I. Scheffler (Eds.), *Logic and Art: Essays in Honor of Nelson Goodman*. Indianapolis, Ind.: Bobbs-Merrill, 1972.

GOODMAN, N. *Languages of Art*. Indianapolis, Ind.: Bobbs-Merrill. 1968.

GOUDGE, T. A. *The Thought of C. S. Peirce*. New York: Dover, 1950.

GREGORY, R. L. *The Intelligent Eye*. New York: McGraw-Hill, 1970.

GYR, J. W. "Is a Theory of Direct Visual Perception Adequate?" *Psychological Bulletin*, 1972, *77*, 246–261.

HAGEN, M. "The Perception of Surface Layout as Pictured in Art." Unpublished memorandum, University of Minnesota, Minneapolis, Minn., 1972.

HAYES, K. J., and HAYES, C. "Picture Perception in a Home-Raised Chimpanzee." *Journal of Comparative and Physiological Psychology*, 1953, *46*, 470–474.

HEBB, D. O. *The Organization of Behavior*. New York: Wiley, 1949.

HELMHOLTZ, H. *Treatise on Physiological Optics*. J. P. S. Southall (Ed). Trans. from 3rd German Edition, Optical Society of America. New York: 1924.

HELSON, H. and BEVAN, W. *Contemporary Approaches to Psychology*. Princeton, N.J.: Van Nostrand, 1967.

HERRNSTEIN, R. J., and LOVELAND, D. H. "Complex Visual Concept in the Pigeon." *Science*, 1964, *146*, 549–551.

HERSKOVITS, M. J. *Man and His Works*. New York: Knopf, 1948.

HESS, E. H. "Ethology and Developmental Psychology." In P. Mussen (Ed.), *Carmichael's Manual of Child Psychology*. New York: Wiley, 1970.

HOCHBERG, J. E. "The Psychophysics of Pictorial Perception." *Audio-Visual Communication Review*, 1962, *10*, 22–54.

HOCHBERG, J. E. *Perception*. Englewood Cliffs, N.J.: Prentice-Hall, 1964.

HOCHBERG, J. E., and BROOKS, V. "Pictorial Recognition as an Unlearned Ability." *American Journal of Psychology*, 1962, *75*, 624–628.

HOFFMAN, C. D. "Recognition Memory for Pictures: A Developmental Study." Paper presented at the Eastern Psychological Association Conference, 1971.

HOGG, J. (Ed.). *Psychology and the Visual Arts*. Harmondsworth, England: Penguin, 1969.

HOWARD, I. P. "An Investigation of a Satiation Process in the Reversible Perspective of Revolving Skeletal Shapes." *Quarterly Journal of Experimental Psychology*, 1961, *13*, 19–33.

HUDSON, W. "Pictorial Depth Perception in Subcultural Groups in Africa." *Journal of Social Psychology*, 1960, *52*, 183–208.

HUDSON, W. "The Study of the Problem of Pictorial Perception Among Unacculturated Groups." *International Journal of Psychology*, 1967, *2*, 89–107.

KAPLAN, G. "Kinetic Disruption of Optical Texture: The Perception of Depth at an Edge." Ph.D. thesis, Cornell University, Ithaca, N.Y., 1969.

KATZ, D. *The World of Color*. Trans. by R. B. MacLeod and C. W. Fox, London: Kegan Paul, 1935.

KENNEDY, J. M. "Lines in Pictures: Are They One-sided?" Paper presented at the Eastern Psychological Association Conference, 1969.

KENNEDY, J. M. "Outlines and Shadows." Paper presented at the American Psychological Association Conference, 1970.

KENNEDY, J. M. "Information and Features in Incomplete Pictures." *Journal of Structural Learning,* 1971, *2,* 73–75.

KENNEDY, J. M. "Perceived Lines Are Not Always the Sums of Their Contours." *Journal of Structural Learning,* 1972, *3,* 7–10.

KENNEDY, J. M. and BRUST, R. "Reversible Figures and Flexibility of Picture Perception." Conference on Cognition and the Arts, F. Perkins School, Mass. 1972.

KENNEDY, J. M. "Misunderstandings of Figure and Ground." *Scandinavian Journal of Psychology* (in press, autumn 1973).

KENNEDY, J. M. "Icons and Information." In D. Olson (Ed.), *National Society for the Study of Education Yearbook* (in press).

KENNEDY, J. M., and FOX, N. "Pictures to See and Pictures to Touch." In D. Perkins and B. Leondar (Eds.) *Art and Cognition* (in preparation).

KIDD, D. *The Essential Kafir.* London: Black, 1904.

KOFFKA, K. *The Growth of the Mind.* New York: Harcourt and Brace, 1925.

KOFFKA, K. *Principles of Gestalt Psychology.* New York: Harcourt and Brace, 1935.

LANGER, S. K. *Philosophy in a New Key.* Cambridge: Harvard University Press, 1951.

LASHLEY, K. S. "The Mechanism of Vision. XV. Preliminary Studies of the Rat's Capacity for Detail Vision." *Journal of General Psychology,* 1935, *46,* 41–73.

LEEPER, R. "A Study of a Neglected Portion of the Field of Learning: The Development of Sensory Organization." *Journal of Genetic Psychology,* 1935, *46,* 41–73.

MACKWORTH, N. H., and BRUNER, J. S. "How Adults and Children Search and Recognize Pictures." *Human Development,* 1970, *13,* 149–177.

MAC LEOD, R. B. "An Experimental Investigation of Brightness-Constancy." *Archives of Psychology,* 1932, *21,* whole no. 135, 19–57.

MAC LEOD, R. B. Personal communication, 1968.

METZGER, W. *Gesetze des Sehens.* Frankfurt am Main: Kramer, 1936.

MILLER, G. A. *Language and Communication.* New York: McGraw-Hill, 1951.

MILLER, R. E. "Experimental Approaches to the Physiological and Behavioral Concomitants of Affective Communication in Rhesus

Monkeys." In S. A. Altmann (Ed.), *Social Communication Among Primates*. Chicago: University of Chicago Press, 1967.

MILLER, R. E., CAUL, W. F. and MIRSKY, I. A. "Communication of Affects Between Feral and Socially Isolated Monkeys." *Journal of Personality and Social Psychology*, 1967, *7*, 231–239.

MORRIS, C. *Signs, Language, and Behavior*. Englewood Cliffs, N.Y.: Prentice-Hall, 1946.

MUNDY-CASTLE, A. C. "Pictorial Depth Perception in Ghanaian Children." *International Journal of Psychology*, 1966, *1*, 289–300.

NADEL, S. F. "A Field Experiment in Racial Psychology." *British Journal of Psychology*, 1937, *28*, 195–211.

NECKER, L. A. "Observations on Some Remarkable Optical Phaenomena Seen in Switzerland; and on an Optical Phaenomenon Which Occurs on Viewing a Figure of a Crystal or Geometrical Solid." *Philosophical Magazine and Journal of Science*, 1832, Third Series, *1*, 329–337.

NEISSER, U. *Cognitive Psychology*. New York: Appleton-Century-Crofts, 1967.

NISSEN, H. W., MACHOVER, S. and KINDER, E. F. "A Study of Performance Tests Given to a Group of Native Negro Children." *British Journal of Psychology*, 1935, *25*, 308–355.

O'CONNOR, N., and HERMELIN, B. "Like and Cross-Modality Recognition in Subnormal Children." *Quarterly Journal of Experimental Psychology*, 1961, *11*, 48–52.

OGDEN, C. K., and RICHARDS, I. A. *The Meaning of Meaning*. New York: Harcourt and Brace, 1946.

PANDINA, R. J., ZELLER, P., and LAWSON, R. B. "Effects of Retinal Disparity Upon Reversible Perspective Figures." Paper presented at the Eastern Psychological Association Conference, 1970.

PAGE, H. W. "Pictorial Depth Perception: A Note." *South African Journal of Psychology*, 1970, *1*, 45–48.

PASTORE, N. *Selective History of Theories of Visual Perception, 1650–1950*. Oxford: Oxford University Press, 1971.

PEIRCE, C. S. *The Philosophy of Peirce*. New York: Routledge and Kegan Paul, 1940.

PERKINS, D. Personal communication, 1970.

PIRENNE, M. H. *Optics, Painting, and Photography*. Cambridge: Cambridge University Press, 1970.

RIVERS, W. H. R. "Observations on the Senses of the Todas." *British Journal of Psychology*, 1904, *1*, 321–396.

RUBIN, E. *Synsoplevede Figurer*. Copenhagen: Gyldendals, 1915.

RUBIN, E. "Figure and Ground" (1915). Partial trans. by M. Wertheimer. In D. C. Beardslee and M. Wertheimer (Eds.), *Readings
in Perception.* New York: Van Nostrand, 1958.

RYAN, T. A. and SCHWARTZ, C. "Speed of Perception as a Function of
Mode of Representation." *American Journal of Psychology,*
1956, *69,* 60–69.

SCHLOSBERG, H. "Stereoscopic Depth from Single Pictures." *American
Journal of Psychology,* 1941, *54,* 601–605.

SEGALL, M. H., CAMPBELL, D. T., and HERSKOVITS, M. J. *The Influence
of Culture on Visual Perception.* New York: Bobbs-Merrill,
1966.

SHAPIRO, M. B. "The Rotation of Drawings by Illiterate Africans."
Journal of Social Psychology, 1960, *52,* 17–30.

SMITH, O. W. "Comparison of Apparent Depth in a Photograph
Viewed from Two Distances." *Perceptual and Motor Skills,*
1958, *8,* 79–81.

SMITH, O. W., and GRUBER, H. "Perception of Depth in Photographs."
Perceptual and Motor Skills, 1958, *8,* 307–313.

SMITH, O. W., SMITH, P. C., and HUBBARD, D. "Perceived Distance as a
Function of the Method of Representing Perspective." *American Journal of Psychology,* 1958, *71,* 662–675.

SMITH, P. C., and SMITH, O. W. "Ball-Throwing Responses to Photo-
graphically Portrayed Targets." *Journal of Experimental Psychology,* 1961, *62,* 223–233.

STEINBERG, S. "The Eye Is a Part of the Mind." *Partisan Review,*
1953, *20,* 194–212.

STONE, L. J., and CHURCH, J. *Childhood and Adolescence,* 2nd ed.
New York: Random House, 1968.

STREET, R. F. *A Gestalt Completion Test.* New York: [Columbia]
Teachers College, 1935.

TAYLOR, B. *Principles of Linear Perspective,* rev. ed., 1935. London:
Taylor, 1715.

VERNON, M. D. *Visual Perception.* London: Cambridge University
Press, 1937.

VICKERS, D. "A Cyclic Decision Model of Perceptual Alternation."
Perception, 1972, *1,* 31–48.

VOGEL, J. M., and TEGHTSOONIAN, M. "The Effects of Perspective Alterations on Apparent Size and Distance Scales." *Perception
and Psychophysics,* 1972, *11,* 294–298.

VON SENDEN, M. *Space and Sight: The Perception of Space and Shape in the Congenitally Blind Before and After Operation.* Trans. by P. Heath, Methuen, London, 1960.

WEINTRAUB, D. J., and WALKER, E. L. *Perception.* Belmont, Calif.: Brooks-Cole, 1966.

WEVER, E. G. "Figure and Ground in the Visual Perception of Form." *American Journal of Psychology,* 1927, *38,* 194–226.

WHITE, B. W., SAUNDERS, F. A., SCADDEN, L., BACH-Y-RITA, P., and COLLINS, C. C. "Seeing with the Skin." *Perception and Psychophysics,* 1970, *7,* 23–27.

WITTGENSTEIN, L. *Tractatus Logico-philosophicus.* London: Routledge and Kegan Paul, 1961.

WOODWORTH, R. S. *Contemporary Schools of Psychology.* New York: Ronald, 1931.

WOODWORTH, R. S. and SCHLOSBERG, H. *Experimental Psychology.* New York: Holt, 1954.

YONAS A., and HAGEN, M. "The Role of Motion Parallax in the Development of Size Constancy." Paper presented at the Society for Research in Child Development Conference, 1971.

ZIMMERMAN, R., and HOCHBERG, J. E. "Pictorial Recognition in the Infant Monkey." *Proceedings of the Psychonomic Society,* 1963, *46* (Abstract). Reported in J. E. Hochberg, *Perception.* Englewood Cliffs, N.J.: Prentice-Hall, 1965.

ZUSNE, L. *Visual Perception of Form.* New York: Academic Press, 1970.

Index

A

Abstractness of pictures, 67
Accuracy of perception, 7, 14-15, 53-55, 156
Aesthetics, 2-4
Africa, subjects from, 65-67, 69-79
ALBERS, J., 148
Ambient optic array, 17; *See also* Optic array
Ambiguity, 9-11, 16, 25, 45, 69-73, 105, 135-136, 140-141, 156-159; of words, 16. *See also* Relevant and irrelevant features of displays
Amodal understanding, 155
Anamorphics, 35-36, 38
Angle subtended, 20-21, 60, 66, 142-143
Anglo-Saxon drawings, 118
ARNHEIM, R., 3, 12, 30-32, 36-37, 49
Art, 4, 45, 86, 155
Artificial sources, 25-27, 37-38, 157
Attention, 7, 9, 63, 88, 139-140; *See also* Figure and ground, Relevant and irrelevant features of displays

B

Background, 110-114; definition of, 111. *See also* Figure and ground, Occlusion, Overlap
BECK, J., 19
Bedouin subjects, 74
BERLYNE, D. E., 3
BERNHEIMER, R., 37, 45-46, 57
BIESHEUVEL, S., 65
Binocular vision, 22-23, 53, 58-60
Blind subjects, 6, 150-154, 158
BOND, E. K., 92
BOTHA, E., 104
BOWER, T. G. R., 58-60, 64
BRAUNSTEIN, M. L., 22
BRODATZ, P., 19
BROOKS, V., 56-57, 79
BRUNER, J. S., 63
BRUST, R., 73, 138-140

C

CAMPBELL, D. T., 66
Captions, 7, 142, 154
Caricature, 2, 28, 41-42, 45, 144-146, 158-159

169